VINDICATED

JENNIFER LeCLAIRE

CHARISMA HOUSE

While the author has made every effort to provide accurate, up-to-date source information at the time of publication, statistics and other data are constantly updated. Neither the publisher nor the author assumes any responsibility for errors or for changes that occur after publication. Further, the publisher and author do not have any control over and do not assume any responsibility for third-party websites or their content.

For more resources like this, visit MyCharismaShop.com and the author's website at jenniferleclaire.org.

Cataloging-in-Publication Data is on file with the Library of Congress.
International Standard Book Number: 978-1-63641-380-8
E-book ISBN: 978-1-63641-381-5

1 2024
Printed in the United States of America

Most Charisma Media products are available at special quantity discounts for bulk purchase for sales promotions, premiums, fundraising, and educational needs. For details, call us at (407) 333-0600 or visit our website at www.charismamedia.com.

The author has made every effort to provide accurate accounts of events, but she acknowledges that others may have different recollections of these events. Some names and identifying details of their stories have been changed to protect the privacy of those individuals.

This book is dedicated to you, the reader. You want vindication, but you are willing to wait on God's timing. You want payback, but you are willing to walk in peace until you see it. You want recompense, but God Himself is your greatest reward. I pray that you will see not only double for your trouble, but triple for your trial—and even a hundredfold return—as you put the principles you learn in this book into practice.

CONTENTS

INTRODUCTION

VINDICATION IS A desire common to man. Whether you are black or white, male or female, young or old, saved or lost, we all experience injustice in our lives. And like the innocent people who suffer at its hand, injustice comes in all shapes and sizes. Indeed, the degrees of injustice range from wounds that never heal to plots that steal, kill, and destroy lives.

In my experience, too many people today live bitter over what happened to them in the past—and, therefore, remain in bondage to a memory that only exists in their mind. That memory acts like a magnet that pulls them back to the familiar emotions of pain, anger, and despair. At the extreme, people pursue an Old Testament ideology of injustice—an eye for an eye, a tooth for a tooth, fracture for fracture, and so on—without understanding that they are only opening a door for the enemy to wreak more havoc in their lives.

There is a better way, and I've found it. It's the way of Jesus, who offers to vindicate us from every injustice. Our heavenly Father promises to make the wrong things right and the crooked places straight. He promises to work all things together for our good if we love Him and stay focused on our purpose instead of our pain. He even promises to take what the enemy meant for harm and turn it around for our good.

I wrote *Vindicated* out of a deep desire to see captives set free and restored. *Vindicated* is based loosely on my life story—and I even produced a short film to inspire you that is available at jenniferleclaire.org. But it's far more than my life story. It's your story in progress. No matter how many times you've been betrayed, overlooked, robbed, or otherwise wronged, God can make it up to you. He *wants* to make it up to you.

Through trials and tragedies, I've learned the secrets of accelerating vindication in my life. I've learned how to apply faith principles to see God avenge me of my adversaries. I've learned to pray without ceasing in the right spirit. I've learned when to go to the courts of heaven. I've learned how to wait on the judge, trusting Him and doing good while He arranges double for my trouble—or more.

If you've picked up this book, it's not an accident. God is moving you closer to the vindication you desire. These biblical principles really work! They are tried and tested. I pray you will be encouraged as you read my story and that vindication becomes the story of your life.

CHAPTER 1

AN EYE FOR AN EYE

WANTED TO SEE her locked up in a prison that had no key. From where I sat in a county jail facing ten years behind bars, Stacy deserved to suffer. She blackmailed me after I rescued her from eviction, and then she called the police on me when I refused to bow to her coercion.

Stacy was the reason I was separated from my baby. Stacy was the reason I had to stay awake all night for fear of being beaten bloody by hardened criminals who saw me as easy prey. And Stacy needed to pay. So there I sat in a cell, scared, hungry, and with nothing but time on my hands, crafting a diabolical plot to take vengeance on Stacy.

Yes, I know. It sounds like the plot of a dark murder mystery. Let me back up and fill in some details. My husband abandoned me and my then-two-year-old daughter in 1999. When I filed for divorce, my attorney gave me shocking news: there was a warrant for my arrest! My divorce attorney urged me to vacate my condo immediately and hire a defense attorney. That one-two punch knocked the wind out of me.

I didn't know many people in Miami Beach, Florida, but my husband and I had befriended a paraplegic Honduran man who we knew only as "Tiny." Because I had nowhere else to turn and nowhere to go, I called Tiny for help. Tiny swiftly connected me with a Colombian family who came to the rescue. Diego, the family patriarch, and his wife sympathized with me. He rented a condo in his company's name for me and my daughter to live in while I sorted things out on the legal front. For a moment, I was able to breathe.

But what happened next caused me to gasp. Diego made me a deal he hoped I couldn't refuse: he offered to have my husband murdered for a "discounted" rate of $5,000. Shocked and frightened for my own life, I called an old friend for help. That old friend, Sam, immediately got in his truck and drove three hundred miles to help me pack up everything I owned in the middle of the night and escape what could have been a deadly situation. Thanks to Sam, I dodged a bullet. I had no idea there was a second bullet in the enemy's chamber, and Stacy, Sam's girlfriend, would soon fire it.

BULLIED AND BLACKMAILED

When I settled into my new apartment, I looked for the best defense attorney money could hire. His legal advice: "This is a paperwork mistake, and the statute of limitations is about to expire. Lay low. Don't worry about it." I followed my attorney's advice. If I could stay under the radar for six months, the whole mess would be behind me. I could put the abandonment and the warrant out of my mind and start picking up the pieces of my broken life. Soon, I landed a major contract with a Fortune 500 company in New York City. My life was starting to turn around—or so I thought.

That's where Stacy comes in. As a single mother working full-time, I needed help packing up to move from Florida to Manhattan. Sam was out of work, so I offered to pay Stacy $500 to help me pack up my apartment. They needed that $500 to pay rent. When Stacy was done, though, she wanted $1,000 instead of $500. When I offered a hard no, she offered a strong threat: "You'll be sorry if you don't give me that money." I was defiant. My husband had just left me. I had a warrant out for my arrest for something I never did, and I was not going to bow to this woman's extortion. I'd had enough!

Then it happened. Two days before I was set to move to New York City, the police came pounding on my door in the middle of the night. I was talking to my friend in Manhattan about the trip when I heard the cops yelling, "Open up! It's the police!" My daughter was sleeping. My dog was barking. My adrenaline was racing. I told my friend to call my mother, who lived about an hour away, and to urge her to come get my daughter so she didn't end up in foster care.

What happened? Stacy knew *America's Most Wanted*—a popular television show featuring reenactments of dangerous fugitives, on-camera interviews, and arrest videos—was in town. Stacy served as a tipster, hoping to gain a cash reward. Just before I was about to start a new life, I was suddenly facing ten years in prison—and I wanted revenge on Stacy.

My vengeance plan was to file a police report naming Stacy as the prime suspect in the theft of large sums of money and jewelry from my apartment. Since her fingerprints were everywhere in my home, I reasoned, she

would wind up behind bars just like me. She would pay.
I pondered it over and over. I decided it was the perfect plot.

I never executed that plan because I found Jesus in
jail. Or I should say, He found me. I turned my life over
to Him. I don't know what happened to Stacy. I forgave her when I got saved and didn't look back. From
where I sit today, I am grateful she called the police on
me. I am grateful I never moved to New York because
my best friend in Manhattan—the one I was talking to
when the police rushed in—was a heroin addict. Instead
of finding salvation, I may have found a deadly addiction
and wound up in hell for eternity. God rescued me, and
He would soon vindicate me.

WE CAN'T PLAY GOD

Despite the flood of emotions that arise in my soul
when I am abused, accused, or otherwise misused, I have
learned that waiting on God's vindication will serve me
better than any feeble attempt I can make to even the
score. God sees everything. That's why I have adopted
a view attributed to Roman Emperor Marcus Aurelius,
"The best revenge is to be unlike him who performed the
injury."[1]

When we try to avenge ourselves—when we try to
punish someone who injured us physically, emotionally, or financially—we are telling God we don't trust
Him. More than that, we are playing God. We are tying
the hands of a just God who wants to make the wrong
things right in our lives. We are walking into the enemy's

self-vindication trap. And we are risking becoming bitter instead of better.

Taking vengeance on your enemies may feel gratifying and satisfying in the heat of the moment. But that feeling is fleeting as it gives way to Holy Spirit conviction. If you avenge yourself, you forfeit God's vindication. And believe me, God's vindication is far better than anything you can gain by striving to prove your enemies wrong or securing carnal payback for the injustice you suffered. God's vindication is worth waiting for.

The late pastor Ray Stedman once pointed to Job as an example of a self-vindicator. Self-vindication, he said, explains the silence of God. "Why does God not help this man? The answer is because he has not yet come to the place where he is willing to listen. As long as a man is defending himself, God will not defend him," Stedman wrote. "There is a theme that runs all through the Bible from beginning to end that says, 'As long as you justify yourself, God will never justify you.' And as long as Job thinks he has some righteous ground on which to stand, God's silence remains. This is true in our lives as well."[2]

REVENGE IS NOT SWEET

When you leave vengeance to God—if you are willing to wait on Him—you will find blessings. It's not always easy, but stand on this promise: "Be strong, do not fear! Behold, your God will come with vengeance, with the recompense of God; He will come and save you" (Isa. 35:4).

When we choose to forgive the person who harmed us, we become more like Christ, "who, when He was reviled, did not revile in return; when He suffered, He did not threaten, but committed Himself to Him who judges righteously" (1 Pet. 2:23). When we refuse to play God, we give Him free rein to work all things for our good.

It's been said that living well is the best revenge. It's difficult to live well—or to do much else for God—when we are wasting precious time plotting and planning to return evil for evil. Peter warned: "Do not repay evil with evil or insult with insult…[but] with blessing, because to this you were called so that you may inherit a blessing" (1 Pet. 3:9, NIV). And Jesus said to love and pray for your enemies. (See Matthew 5:44.)

When you leave the vengeance to God, you will see healing and restoration in your life. An old Dutch proverb says, "The tree of revenge does not carry fruit." I disagree. I believe the tree of revenge carries rotten fruit. But the tree of forgiveness yields the fruit of emotional healing. English philosopher, statesman, scientist, lawyer, jurist, author, and pioneer Francis Bacon put it this way, "A man that studieth revenge, keeps his own wounds green, which otherwise would heal, and do well."[3] Your emotional well-being is connected to forgiveness, and so is God's justice.

AN EYE FOR AN EYE?

In the Book of Leviticus, we see a tit-for-tat form of retribution. An eye for an eye. A tooth for a tooth. A fracture for a fracture. A life for a life. But Jesus tells us not to resist an evil person (Matt. 5:39). We are supposed to turn the other cheek and walk the extra mile. That takes self-control and spiritual maturity, but God always gives us the grace to obey His commands. I could testify to this over and over again. But I'll tell you one remarkable story.

About a year after I left a spiritually abusive church—and was emotionally terrorized because the leadership was afraid I'd expose them—people came to me to share how they witnessed the public attacks against me on social media. More than that, they said they witnessed how I never retaliated or even defended myself. My response spoke volumes to them about who was moving in the right spirit and in the wrong spirit. That was a measure of vindication, and that was just the beginning. God promoted me time and time again while their influence diminished.

Be the bigger person. Francis Bacon put it this way: "In taking revenge, a man is but even with his enemy; but in passing it over, he is superior."[4] God is the biggest person. He is your vindicator. Next time you are wronged, launch into prayer.

In his classic devotional *My Utmost for His Highest*, the late Oswald Chambers said our passion for vindication distracts us. He wrote: "St. Augustine prayed, 'O Lord, deliver me from this lust of always vindicating myself.' Such a need for constant vindication destroys our soul's faith in God."[5] We need to walk in love, even with those who have harmed us as love "is not self-seeking" (1 Cor. 13:5, NIV).

I find Psalm 17 especially helpful: "Hear a just cause, O LORD, attend to my cry; give ear to my prayer which is not from deceitful lips. Let my vindication come from Your presence; let Your eyes look on the things that are upright" (vv. 1–2). If you have taken revenge on your enemies, repent before God and ask Him to pick up your case again. He is merciful.

CHAPTER 2

GOD IS YOUR VINDICATOR

I NEVER HIT THAT cop, much less resisted arrest with violence. But one dishonest police officer falsely accused me and arrested me on trumped-up charges—and it just about destroyed my life.

I was in my early twenties when my fiancé came home from work in a nasty mood one afternoon. One unkind word led to another, and I soon found myself ducking a bowl of macaroni that was spiraling toward my head. It missed me but left a hole in the wall, and I was shocked and scared. He had never been violent before. "Calm down, or I'll call the police," I warned.

Long story short, he didn't calm down. I ran into our bedroom, locked the door, and called the police. My fingers trembled as I punched in the three numbers I hoped would send a rescue squad: 9-1-1. Unfortunately, my fiancé busted through the door and put his hands on me. I scratched and clawed to get away just as the police arrived on the scene and came pounding on the door.

A female officer called us both outside. She ordered me to sit on the curb while she took my clean-cut fiancé about ten feet away to question him. Of course, he lied to save his own hide, swearing to the officer that I had hit him without provocation. She believed him because there was a scratch on his arm—and because I had a bald head with a long lock of hair dangling over my right eye, several tattoos, and a pierced eyebrow.

Suddenly things took a sharp turn for the worse. Barefoot and wearing only shorts and a tank top, I scooted over a couple inches to escape the army of hungry ants snacking on my ankles. With this slight movement, the officer went ballistic and barreled toward me with fierce anger in her eyes as the male officer was putting my fiancé in a squad car.

It was all surreal. Concerned for his fate, I began protesting—even begging the officers not to take him to jail. And just that quickly, injustice reared its ugly head. The female officer grabbed me and forcibly escorted me to her squad car. I didn't understand what was happening. I was the victim here. I was the one who called the police.

FALSELY ACCUSED AND ABUSED

"Calm down, or I'll say you hit me!" the female officer threatened. "What?" I questioned. "You can't do that! I haven't done anything!" Famous last words. The next thing I knew, I was being body slammed against the back of a police car and assaulted. In tears, I begged her to stop, but the merciless beating continued. She beat my arms, legs, and back. I had bruises over much of my body that took weeks to start fading away. The damage to my soul would take longer to heal.

Since I would not press charges against my fiancé, they had no choice but to let him go. Not so for me. I was charged with two felonies: battery on a law enforcement officer and resisting arrest with violence, which came with a ten-year prison sentence and a $5,000 fine. The drama and trauma sent me into such a deep depression that I didn't even fight the charges. I pled no contest and agreed to probation.

A year later, things began to improve. My fiancé and I moved about four hundred miles south to start a new life. Despite receiving official court authorization to move—I even took my mother with me to the probation office to make sure all the paperwork was in order—there was a mix-up somewhere. The paperwork was apparently lost in the system.

Of course, I didn't know that. The officer told me it may take several months before they assigned me a new probation officer in South Florida. Basically, they said, "Don't call us; we'll call you." They had my new address and my phone number, so I left and didn't look back. Within a few months, I was married, pregnant, and had started a new life. I wouldn't find out that there was a warrant for my arrest for violation of probation until my husband abandoned me and I was about to go to divorce court.

The high-dollar attorney I hired assured me the matter was a paperwork issue and would be easily cleared up if the statute of limitations didn't run out first. You know the rest of the story. Stacy turned me in for reward money after I wouldn't bow to her bribes. But what I haven't told you is my attorney went missing for five days. I sat in jail with no defense for nearly a week. I was simultaneously panicky and livid. When my attorney finally did show up for the bail hearing, I was denied bond. They would not let me go home.

In fact, the same judge denied me bail three times, even with a stipulation of home arrest and an agreement to wear an ankle bracelet. My two-year-old daughter had lost her father and was now in danger of losing her mother too, as the heartless district attorney sought to make an example out of me. The high-dollar attorney—the same one who told me this was a simple paperwork issue—was now urging me to take a five-year prison plea deal. I was numb and didn't know where to turn.

WHEN I WAS IN JAIL, JESUS VISITED ME

Allow me to fast-forward from the gory details to the glorious details. A group of evangelists came to the jail with testimonies of hard knocks. I found hope in Jesus and accepted Him as my Savior. A few days later, the Holy Spirit made it crystal clear I would be released on the fortieth day of my captivity. That didn't seem possible since I couldn't even get out on bail, and the judge on my case was on vacation until well past the fortieth day. But, as I found out, nothing is impossible with God.

I didn't know much of the Word, and I had no teaching about God being my vindicator, but He gave me the gift of faith. Over and over, the Holy Spirit confirmed my release on the fortieth day. And I believed it. I told everyone who would listen, even though they were skeptical. I kept confessing freedom was coming. Faith was rising. I was convinced it would be just as God said. Nobody could tell me otherwise.

Suddenly things started turning in my favor. My

grandmother found an attorney who saw the injustice and agreed to fight for me. His first words to me were, "How long have you been here?" When I told him I'd been there for twenty days, he retorted, "You won't be here more than another twenty days."

Hiring my freedom-fighting attorney cost me almost every penny I had—about $70,000—but I never had to stand before the disagreeable judge again. And I was released on the fortieth day, just like God told me. The felony charges against me were dropped, and my name was cleared. But His vindication didn't end there.

Over time, God also restored every penny the devil stole from me through legal fees or otherwise. He restored my freelance writing client base tenfold. He directed my steps to an oceanfront condo and told me He would pay the rent. I could go on and on about God's vindication in my life. In fact, if there is one theme that's run throughout my life, it has been the vindication of God. Hallelujah!

GOD IS YOUR VINDICATOR

Here's the good news: God is no respecter of persons (Acts 10:34). If He vindicated me, He will vindicate you. If He restored what the devil stole from me, He will restore what the devil stole from you. (See Proverbs 6:31.) I challenge you right now: instead of complaining day and night about what the enemy has done in your life, try praying day and night for God's justice.

Are you desperate enough to see God's justice in your life that you'll persist in day-and-night prayer until you see Him move? Will you stand like the woman who petitioned the unjust judge and believe that God will avenge

His elect speedily when we pray in faith? (See Luke 18:7–8.) Do you believe God is your vindicator? Is anything too hard for God? (See Jeremiah 32:26–27.)

I don't know who has maligned you, who has done you dirty, or what the enemy has stolen from you. But I am absolutely confident of this: God is your vindicator. If you believe it and you persist in prayer for justice with faith and patience, you will see God's vindicating power make the wrong things right and the crooked places straight in your life. Only believe.

In his book *I Declare: 31 Promises to Speak Over Your Life*, Joel Osteen wrote, "God will vindicate you for the wrongs that have been done. He will pay you back for unfair situations. He promised He will not only bring your dreams to pass but He will give you even the secret desires of your heart. Dare to trust Him. Come back to that place of peace. Quit being worried, stressed out, wondering if it will happen. God has you in the palm of His hand. He has never once failed before, and the good news is He is not about to start now."[1]

So how do you get to know God as your vindicator? Start with getting to know His heart for you and His faithfulness toward you. When you grow in the grace and knowledge of our Lord and Savior Jesus Christ, you will more clearly see Him as vindicator. (See 2 Peter 3:18.) If you seek to know Him as your vindicator through His promises and accounts of vindication in Scripture, you will come to expect His vindication because vindication of the righteous is one of His ways.

Unfortunately, though, when it comes to knowing God as vindicator, there is no substitute for tasting His vindicating power for yourself. David knew God was his vindicator because he experienced vindication over and over again. In Psalm 62:5–7, David said this: "I depend on God alone; I put my hope in him. He alone protects and saves me; he is my defender, and I shall never be defeated. My salvation and honor depend on God; he is my strong protector; he is my shelter" (GNT).

CHAPTER 3

THE VINDICATOR'S PROMISES

VINDICATION IS THE story of my life. In fact, there aren't enough pages in this book to tell about the many wrongs I've suffered—and the vindication I've witnessed in the aftermath of those wrongs. I'll sprinkle more inspiring stories of God's vindicating power in my life in the chapters ahead, but first I want to build up your faith by showing you the many vindication promises in God's Word.

With this firm foundation, you'll be equipped to overcome the battle in your mind that tempts you to vindicate yourself and forfeit God's payback. Consider Peter's bold words in 2 Peter 1:4, "And because of his glory and excellence, he has given us great and precious promises" (NLT). Did you catch that? His promises are both great and precious. Indeed, Paul said all of God's promises are yes and amen in Christ (2 Cor. 1:20).

Moses made it clear, "God is not a man, so he does not lie. He is not human, so he does not change his mind. Has he ever spoken and failed to act? Has he ever promised and not carried it through?" (Num. 23:19, NLT). Of course, the answer is a resounding "No!" God's promises in His Word do not return void, but they accomplish what they are sent to do (Isa. 55:11). God watches over His Word in your life to perform it (Jer. 1:12).

If you need vindication, God will supply it. Under the inspiration of the Holy Spirit, Paul wrote, "My God shall supply all your need according to His riches in glory by Christ Jesus" (Phil. 4:19). Rest assured, God hasn't forgotten your need—or His promise—of vindication in your life. And He has creative ways of vindicating you. Let these vindication promises strengthen you in the midst of this trial.

YOUR VINDICATOR IS NEAR

Rachel was barren and bullied—but this same Rachel was also vindicated. Rachel said, "'God has vindicated me, and He has also heard my voice and has given me a son.' Therefore she called his name Dan" (Gen. 30:6, MEV). If people have teased you or looked down on you because of what you don't have, remember Rachel—and remember God's vindication promises.

Isaiah penned this Messianic prophecy concerning Jesus: "He who vindicates me is near; who will contend with me? Let us stand up to each other. Who is my adversary? Let him come near to me." (Isa. 50:8, MEV). Remember, when you are in the midst of the pain of being wronged, the vindicator is near. He will deal with your adversaries in His perfect timing.

His body filled with sores, Job sorely needed vindication. He confidently wrote, "Behold now, I have prepared my case; I know that I will be vindicated" (Job 13:18, NASB). You can have faith that vindication is your portion no matter what case the enemy has against you. If you are in the right, God will make it right. Be sure to stay in right standing with God by submitting to His Word.

Moses assured us, "For the LORD will vindicate His people, and will have compassion on His servants, when He sees that their strength is gone, and there is none remaining, bond or free" (Deut. 32:36, NASB). You may feel like you can't go on because the pain you feel is too great. But you can keep standing. God is able to make you stand while you wait for His vindication. Is anything too hard for God? (See Jeremiah 32:27.)

Jeremiah, known as the weeping prophet, wrote: "The LORD has brought about our vindication; come and let us recount in Zion the work of the LORD our God!" (Jer. 51:10, NASB). Has God vindicated you in the past? It's always good to encourage yourself in the Lord, remembering your past vindications. Know that if He did it once, He will do it again!

MAGNIFY THE LORD

David walked in consistent vindication. Like me, vindication was the story of David's life. He once prayed, "Vindicate me, O God, and plead my cause against an ungodly nation; deliver me from the deceitful and unjust man" (Ps. 43:1, MEV). Let this be your prayer. The Holy Spirit is your advocate. He will vindicate you in the face of harassment, just like He vindicated David from Saul's murderous plots.

David was certain: "He will bring forth your righteousness as the light, and your judgment as the noonday" (Ps. 37:6, MEV). Rest assured, the light of God's vindication will rest upon you. And remember, when you are persecuted for righteousness' sake, His glory is already upon you. (See 1 Peter 4:14.) Bask in His glory and love until you see your promised vindication.

Once again, David prayed for God's vindicating power: "Save me, O God, by Your name, and vindicate me by Your power" (Ps. 54:1, NASB). Remember, it's not by might, not by power, but by His Spirit that you will be vindicated. (See Zechariah 4:6.) You can pray without ceasing, but you can't rush the manifestation of the vindication promises.

David also testified: "For You have maintained my right and my cause; You sat on the throne judging righteously" (Ps. 9:4, AMPC). When it seems like your vindication will never manifest, remind yourself that God is a righteous judge. He will maintain your rights and your cause. He will not let the enemy get away with harming you.

Once again, David prayed: "Vindicate me, O LORD, for I have walked in my integrity, and I have trusted in the LORD without wavering" (Ps. 26:1, NASB). While you are standing on the promise, walk with integrity. Walk in truth. Be honest and fair with others. Don't act like the one who wronged you.

"Let them shout for joy and rejoice, who favor my vindication; and let them say continually, 'The LORD be magnified, who delights in the prosperity of His servant'" (Ps. 35:27, NASB). Go ahead and magnify the Lord over the injustice you faced, knowing that since God delights in your prosperity, He will make a way for your vindication even when there seems to be no way. He's the God of miracles!

VINDICATION IS ON THE WAY

Now, Paul wrote, because we have these promises, let us cleanse ourselves from everything that can defile our body or spirit. (See 2 Corinthians 7:1.) If you believe God's promises of vindication, act like it.

If you truly believe God is your vindicator, stop letting your anger escort you into sinful behavior. Stop telling everybody what "they" did to you. Stop feeling sorry for yourself. Instead, stand on the vindication promises. Write them out and put them inside your shoes if you have to! Confess God's vindication promises. War with them. And wait for them to manifest. Your vindication is surely coming.

It may feel like the Lord is taking His sweet time to fulfill your vindication promises. But keep this in mind: He may be trying to work something out in you before He delivers you to a bountiful table in the presence of your enemies. Remember, while you wait on vindication, work out your salvation with fear and trembling. (See Philippians 2:12.) God's vindication is worth waiting for.

CHAPTER 4

ONLY BELIEVE

I HAD TO MAKE a choice that would change the course of my life—and my attorney only presented me with two options: I could take a plea deal and potentially go home in three and a half years with good behavior, or I could risk spending ten years behind bars. There was no third choice. My attorney offered no possibility of vindication despite his bold pre-hire promises.

After experiencing the horrors of confinement for nearly three weeks—and after experiencing salvation that promised eternal life—I decided a plea deal was my only option. I was about to sign the papers when my grandma fired my high-dollar lawyer and swept in with a freedom-fighting attorney.

With a paperback small print Bible in hand, I started eating the Word. (Lord knows I wasn't eating anything else. I traded my food every day for protection from jailhouse bullies.) As I read the Word, the Holy Spirit began speaking to me. He showed me through Scripture and later spoke to my heart that I would be released in forty days.

Being a new convert, I had no idea that the number forty was a symbol of testing and trial, but every time I opened my Bible, I randomly landed on passages about

Moses' forty years in Egypt or the Israelites' forty years in the desert or the forty-day flood Noah endured or Jesus' forty days of temptation in the wilderness. Of course, it wasn't random at all.

After several days of this supernatural guidance through the Word, the Holy Spirit made God's will clear—and I told everyone I would go home on the fortieth day. Nobody believed me. It seemed impossible, considering the judge had refused to allow me out on bail three times. And how could it happen with the judge on vacation well after the fortieth day of my captivity?

All I can say is, "But God." On the fortieth day, I was called into a holding cell with other inmates to face a new judge on the case, but *the* judge—Jesus Christ—is not a man that He should lie. I never stood before an earthly judge to hear my case. I was never tried or convicted by my accusers. I was released on the fortieth day, just like the Holy Spirit told me I would be. I was vindicated.

With that as my foundation story in Christ, I've never struggled to believe God to vindicate me. In fact, I've come to the place where—at least most of the time—I can lay aside the flood of emotions and sincerely rejoice when someone wrongs me because I know vindication and payback are coming. I've experienced vindication far too many times for the enemy to talk me out of my faith for justice and restoration in the wake of the enemy's brute force attacks.

BUILDING UP YOUR FAITH

Maybe you've never experienced vindication. Maybe you've been waiting for a long, long time. Maybe it's hard for you to believe your vindication will ever manifest. Maybe you are about to give up on the vindication promises of God. If that rings at all true, don't fret because of evildoers. Build your faith for vindication instead. So how do you develop faith for vindication? There are more ways than one.

If you've tasted God's vindication in the past—even the smallest morsel of vindication—remind yourself how God made the crooked places straight. This was one of David's strategies. Goliath cursed David by his gods, but David remembered his past victories over the lions and the bears who came to devour his sheep. David knew God would vindicate Israel from the giant. Experience builds faith.

You also build faith for vindication by reading and confessing Scriptures about vindication, as we did in the last chapter, and reading accounts of God vindicating His people. We know "faith comes by hearing and hearing by the word of God" (Rom. 10:17). When you hear yourself speaking the Word of God, it stirs your spirit and renews your mind at the same time. It's a one-two punch against doubt and unbelief.

But take Romans 10:17 a step further. Meditate on the Word of God.

This is a time-tested strategy Joshua deployed. Meditating on God's vindication promises—thinking about them, talking about them, and even memorizing them—paves the way for your breakthrough. God told Joshua, "This Book of the Law shall not depart from your mouth, but you shall meditate in it day and night, that you may observe to do according to all that is written in it. For then you will make your way prosperous, and then you will have good success" (Josh. 1:8).

But don't stop there. Listen to the testimonies of those who have witnessed miraculous vindications. You can watch a film of my story at jenniferleclaire.org. Warning: It's a tearjerker.

GOD WILL HANG YOUR HAMAN

You know Esther's "such a time as this" story, but her cousin Mordecai's vindication is an important subplot in the historical drama. When Ahasuerus, king of Persia, couldn't sleep one night, he curled up with the chronicles of his kingdom. As his servant was reading the accounts, Ahasuerus heard of a man named Mordecai who saved his life by reporting an assassination attempt. The king was grateful and wanted to honor Mordecai, so he called in his right-hand man, Haman, for some ideas.

King Ahasuerus had no idea the depths of hatred Haman harbored toward Mordecai. He didn't know Mordecai had once refused to bow to Haman in homage. He didn't know Haman was so offended by Mordecai that he plotted not only to destroy the Jewish man but all Jews everywhere. Indeed, Haman had Mordecai's entire race on a hit list.

In an ironic twist, Haman was entering the court to ask the king to have Mordecai hanged when Ahasuerus asked him a question, "What shall be done for the man whom the king delights to honor?" (Est. 6:6). Haman figured he was up for a promotion and offered a suggestion. We read this in Esther 6:7–10:

For the man whom the king delights to honor, let a royal robe be brought which the king has worn, and a horse on which the king has ridden, which has a royal crest placed on its head. Then let this robe and horse be delivered to the hand of one of the king's most noble princes, that he may array the man whom the king delights to honor.

Then parade him on horseback through the city square, and proclaim before him: "Thus shall it be done to the man whom the king delights to honor!" Then the king said to Haman, "Hurry, take the robe and the horse, as you have suggested, and do so for Mordecai the Jew who sits within the king's gate! Leave nothing undone of all that you have spoken."

That's vindication!

Mordecai ultimately received a greater vindication. After Haman was exposed, we read the end of the story: "For Mordecai was great in the king's palace, and his fame spread throughout all the provinces; for this man Mordecai became increasingly prominent" (Est. 9:4).

CHRONICLES OF VINDICATION

Of course, Scripture chronicles story after story showcasing God's vindicating power. You'll recall how Joseph's jealous brothers threw him in a pit and left him to die before changing their minds and selling him as a slave to an Egyptian named Potiphar.

Soon, Potiphar's wife tried to seduce the young prophet, and when he refused her advances, she falsely accused him of rape. Joseph was thrown into prison. All told, Joseph suffered thirteen years before God vindicated him and established him as prime minister of Egypt—the second-most powerful man in the world. (See Genesis 41:37–57.)

Then there's Hannah, whose husband's "other wife" constantly needled her because she was barren. Hannah was so miserable she wept instead of eating (1 Sam. 1:6–7). Making matters worse, her husband, Elkanah, couldn't understand her pain: "Hannah, why do you weep? Why do you not eat? And why is your heart grieved? Am I not better to you than ten sons?" (1 Sam. 1:8).

When Hannah petitioned God over her barrenness in the temple, the High Priest Eli saw her lips moving but heard no sound—and had the audacity to accuse her of being drunk! I can't imagine the sting of his words. But God heard Hannah's cries and vindicated her in front of Eli and Elkanah's "other wife." God opened her womb—and Hannah gave birth to Samuel, one of the greatest prophets of all time. (See 1 Samuel 1–2).

God vindicated Job when he prayed for his friends. God vindicated David when he fought Goliath, when he ran from Saul, and when his son Absalom launched an insurrection that forced him to leave Jerusalem barefoot and weeping. God vindicated Samson, whose eyes the Philistines had mercilessly gouged out. God vindicated Jacob after Laban's bait-and-switch deal that left him with Leah instead of Rachel and forced him into another seven years of hard labor under unjust circumstances.

God vindicated Leah, whose husband loved another woman more than she, by making her womb fruitful. She birthed most of the tribes of Israel. God vindicated Moses when his siblings questioned his authority. God vindicated Noah when the rain came and flooded an unbelieving earth. And God vindicated Jesus, His sinless Son, who died on a cross to pave the way for our eternal vindication.

It's not a matter of *if* God will vindicate the righteous. It's a matter of *when*. If you build your faith and wait on God, His vindication may shine down on you sooner than you think—and it will be sweeter than you can imagine. Psalm 37:6 assures us, "He will bring forth your righteousness as the light and your judgment as the noonday" (NASB). Let Job 13:18 be your confession: "Behold now, I have prepared my case; I know that I will be vindicated" (AMP).

CHAPTER 5

DO YOUR PART

BEFORE I LAUNCHED a successful journalism career—and long before I became the first-ever female editor of *Charisma* magazine—I had my heart set on being a film editor. I was the one who sat in the auditorium until the last credit rolled off the black screen. I imagined seeing my name among the actors, directors, and lighting technicians.

But when I enrolled in college, I wasn't allowed to take editing classes—or even film classes—straightaway. There were conditions. In the college world, those conditions are called prerequisites. Even though I wanted to be a film editor, I had to take classes that were not directly related to film editing.

I had to take English and math classes. I had to take theater, stagecraft, and entertainment technology classes. I had to take audio production classes, stage lighting classes, and camera technique classes. At the time, it seemed like a lot of work to get what I ultimately wanted—the film editing classes. But there was no other way through. I had to meet the requirements. I had to take the prerequisites. I had to wait.

God has promised vindication throughout His Word.

More than mere promises, we've seen clear evidence of how God has vindicated people throughout the pages of the Bible, from Job to Hannah to David and beyond. And God's ancient vindication promises are still relevant in modern times. Real-life Christians today—including me—have tremendous testimonies about God's yes-and-amen promises of vindication. If we meet His conditions for vindication, we will see vindication. It's just a matter of time.

So what are the prerequisites—the conditions—for vindication? What does God expect from us? We know we're not supposed to take matters into our own hands. But while we wait on God for vindication, how do we position ourselves for the manifestation of the promise? Well, it starts with forgiveness, then progresses to praying for your enemies, blessing your enemies, and, sometimes even letting yourself or God off the blame hook.

FORGIVENESS BEFORE VINDICATION

When I raced out of my house to drive to a local ministry assignment, God arranged a pit stop—a divine appointment—I wasn't expecting. My low fuel light started nagging me. Even though I was running late, I couldn't ignore the yellow light on the dashboard warning me to stop and refuel. When I pulled off the highway to find a gas station, I learned a lesson about forgiveness I'll never forget.

Out of nowhere, a stranger fueling his car at the opposite pump started complaining to me about his life—and his ex-wife. As he told the story, his "wicked, cheating wife" had "stolen everything he worked for his whole life" in what sounded like an especially nasty divorce. I could almost taste his bitterness as he shared how she had used him, abused him, and turned his children against him. He seemed to grow angrier with each word he spoke, as if he was reliving the injustice in real time. He was fuming.

I wasn't sure what he might do next, so I politely disengaged—but he would not stop. Suddenly I had a revelation: The Holy Spirit ordered my steps to this gas station to give him a word of life. I forcefully interrupted him and told him part of my own story. I told him how my husband ran off with a woman about half his age when our daughter was only two years old and paid no child support. I told him how I was falsely accused of a crime I didn't commit and ended up in jail for forty days and lost everything I had, including my life savings, my apartment, my job, and my dog.

The man listened intently, waiting for his turn to speak again. He was ready to kick off an official pity party with me as his first guest, but I didn't give him that chance. I asked him if he was a Christian. He said he was, "but…" I asked him if he understood the power of forgiveness. He said he did, "but…" I didn't let him keep giving me his bitter buts. I told him if I forgive, he could. I told him that if Christ forgave him, he was obliged to forgive others.

I told him Jesus said, "For if you forgive men their trespasses, your heavenly Father will also forgive you. But if you do not forgive men their trespasses, neither will your Father forgive your trespasses" (Matt. 6:14–15). I don't know if he forgave his ex-wife or not. I only know he stopped telling his story. He looked down to the ground in silence for a while, got in his car, and drove away. My assignment there was finished.

If we don't forgive others, our prayers for vindication won't reach the throne room of God. Forgive from your heart, understanding that your emotions may not immediately change. Forgiveness is not an emotion; it's a decision of our will. You won't experience vindication with unforgiveness in your heart. On the contrary, you will get bitter instead of better like the fuming man at the gas station.

LOVE YOUR ENEMIES

Loving your enemies is a tall order. But Jesus made a clear command in Matthew 5:44: "Love your enemies." That's easier said than done, but God's grace is sufficient for you to obey. I'll admit it. I tried to get out of loving my enemies. I even looked through every Bible translation, hoping it would offer a more palatable command, but every rendition of Matthew 5:44 says the same thing in just about the same way!

Still hoping for a way of escape, I looked up the Greek word for "love" in that verse. I discovered the word for love is *agape*. Agape is God's own love. Wait, what? We're supposed to love our enemies the way God loves us. That means unconditional love. We are commanded to love them despite the trouble and pain they caused us through their lying, stealing, treacherous behavior that broke our hearts or left us destitute. The word *agape* in Matthew 5:44 means "to welcome, to entertain, to be fond of, to love dearly."[1] You may think that's asking a lot, but while we were yet sinners Christ died for us because of agape (Rom. 5:8).

The command to love our enemies may mean God has to do deep work in us before we get the vindication we so desperately desire. This was true of Joseph. The son of Jacob and Rachel started out as a teenager, reporting his brothers' misdeeds to a dad who was already giving him special treatment. Joseph also bragged to his brothers—not once but twice—about prophetic dreams God gave him in which the eleven young men were bowing down to him.

God allowed Joseph's brothers to throw him into a pit, sell him as a slave, and fake his death. He was later falsely accused of rape and sent to prison for at least two years before he received his ultimate vindication and was promoted to prime minister of Egypt. In the end, when Joseph could have had his brothers killed, "he comforted them and spoke kindly to them" (Gen. 50:21). Though it took him some time to get there, Joseph ultimately showed them agape—he welcomed, entertained, was fond of, and loved them dearly—after Israel passed away.

PRAY FOR THOSE WHO WRONGED YOU

When people use us, abuse us, and accuse us, we often have a knee-jerk reaction. We get angry and may "vent" to people. We may choose to defend ourselves and accuse the accuser. But that's a mistake because, in doing so, we are taking vengeance into our own hands. If you need to tell one or two people what someone did to you for the sake of prayer and counsel, I believe that is permissible in the Lord's eyes. But we should not use our mouths to return evil for evil. We should use our mouths to pray.

Jesus said, "Pray for them which despitefully use you, and persecute you" (Matt. 5:44, KJV). How do you pray for people who wrong you, you ask? Some pray that God would rebuke them or lift up "get 'em God!" prayers. That's not the right spirit. You need to move in the opposite spirit. When you pray for those who spitefully use you, you need to get to a place where you can pray for them like you would your closest friend.

Admittedly, that's not easy at first. But if you stick with it, you will get there. God will give you grace to pray rightly when you obey. You'll start to take pity on your persecutors, knowing they are going to reap what they sowed if they don't repent. You'll tap into God's heart for them, which is for restoration. You'll stop being the judge and start being the intercessor.

The late Martin Luther King Jr. wrote these wise words: "Returning hate for hate multiplies hate, adding deeper darkness to a night already devoid of stars. Darkness cannot drive out darkness; only light can do that. Hate cannot drive out hate; only love can do that."[2]

BLESS THOSE WHO HAVE CURSED YOU

Jesus gave us another command in the Sermon on the Mount that's difficult for many people to practice: "Bless those who curse you" (Matt. 5:44). Let's put this into perspective. To bless someone, essentially, is to say good things about them. By contrast, to curse is to say evil things about them.

Some people pray imprecatory prayers against those

who have done them wrong. Imprecatory prayers are also known as cursing prayers—and we often find David praying them in the Psalms. David prayed for his enemy's teeth to be broken and for their names to be blotted out of the Book of Life. Intense!

But we have a revelation David didn't: We're not wrestling against flesh and blood, not really (Eph. 6). Although the enemy may inspire flesh and blood— difficult people—to harm us, we must direct our warfare prayers against the enemy, binding his hand in our lives while blessing the people who are under his sway. I say it this way, "Bless the people. Bind the devil." When you do, you maintain your authority in the spirit because you are acting like Jesus, who delegated His authority to you.

Ask God to bless them, give them revelation, and help them receive His love. Bless their family. Bless their finances. Bless their bodies. Bless their minds. Bless their spirits. Stand in a posture of blessing, and you'll find God's blessings in your life. Sow blessings and reap blessings. First Peter 3:9 tells us, "Not returning evil for evil or reviling for reviling, but on the contrary blessing, knowing that you were called to this, that you may inherit a blessing."

FORGIVE YOURSELF

We started off talking about forgiving others. But you may also need to forgive yourself. You may be beating yourself up for not discerning the betrayer. You may feel guilty for losing the money. You may be fighting off condemnation for dating—or even marrying—the wrong person.

You have to forgive yourself. Acknowledge you made a mistake, ask God to forgive you, and then let it go. God chooses to remember your sin no more (Jer. 31:34), and so should you. If you hurt someone with your poor decision, apologize and make amends if you can. Look for the lesson and ask God to help you not make the same mistake again. Cast the care on the Lord because He cares for you. (See 1 Peter 5:7.)

LET GOD OFF THE HOOK

Sometimes we blame God when bad things happen to us. We may not even realize we're doing it. It can be subtle. You think, "Well, God should have told me not to get involved in that deal." The reality is, He probably did, but perhaps you missed His still small voice—or were just dead set on what you wanted. If you want God to vindicate you, you can't blame Him for your mistakes.

When Job was going through his trial, he lost everything. He lost his family, his livestock, his barns, and his health. He lost it all. His wife said, "Curse God and die!" (Job 2:8). But Job refused to blame God for his losses. He didn't put God on the hook, even though he didn't understand what was happening. His stance was, "Though He slay me, yet will I trust Him" (Job 13:15).

God never does anything that requires forgiveness. He is perfect in all of His ways. Many people cry out, "Why, God, why?" Jesus told us why in John 10:10, "The thief comes only in order to steal and kill and destroy. I came that they may have and enjoy life, and have it in abundance [to the full, till it overflows]" (AMP).

If you want overflowing vindication, you can't blame

God for the bad things that have happened to you. "Well, He allowed the enemy to touch Job. He allowed this to happen to me." In a sense, yes, nothing happens outside of God's control. But the other side of it is, you have free will. If we are not vigilant, that enemy of ours, the devil, will do whatever we allow him to do. God has given us authority over the enemy and has promised to give us wisdom if we ask for it. Nothing is ever God's fault. He's a good Father.

CHAPTER 6

SHEDDING THE VICTIM MENTALITY

I HAD JUST TURNED thirty. I was traumatized. And I was standing at a crossroads in life—a life radically different from a short six weeks earlier when I was married and had a thriving journalism career. I was not only practically penniless, but now I was suddenly homeless. The vindication celebration that saw me dance my way out of jail after forty days of fighting for my freedom quickly turned into mourning.

When my parents picked me up from jail, they didn't take me back to my apartment. They took me to their house. I wondered what was going on until my father told me he had broken the lease on my apartment. He was convinced I was going to prison for ten years. If that weren't disappointing enough, he also gave away my loyal companion, a Dalmatian that had been with me through all the trauma and drama of the past six life-altering months.

I was forced to live with my parents. Soon, I felt like I was in a different kind of prison. My parents were not serving the Lord at the time, and the atmosphere in the house was tense. Within a few months, I spent what little money I had to move to a small town in another state and start my life over. That decision didn't solve my problems. In fact, I found myself on food stamps, living on Barely Getting By Street for the next thirteen months.

In that season, I had a decision to make. I could focus on all the bad things people did to me—my husband's choice to abandon me and our daughter, the piles of debt he left behind, the police encounter that bruised my body and scarred my soul—or I could choose to trust a God I barely knew to make a way out of no way. Put another way, I could choose to be a victim or a victor. I chose to break the victim mentality and walk in victory. And it wasn't a once-and-for-all choice. The voice of victimhood revisited me from time to time—and still does. Like you, I've had to learn to resist it and cast it down.

You've probably faced devastating circumstances that set you up for a fall or set you back for years. Maybe you were cheated on, betrayed, lied to, or stolen from. In that moment of turmoil when the enemy is working to victimize you, you too are at a crossroads in life. You have to choose: Will you forgive and come up higher, or will you adopt a victim mentality, wallow in self-pity, and allow the enemy to continue robbing you of God's plans for a future and hope—and vindication? (See Jeremiah 29:11.)

YOU ARE NOT A VICTIM

The good news is no matter what has happened to you, God doesn't see you as a victim. He sees you as more than a conqueror in Christ (Rom. 8:37). And He offers divine and practical wisdom on conquering the victim mentality that often manifests while you wait for vindication.

Indeed, we see people throughout Scripture battling the victim mentality. The man with the illness for thirty-eight years is a prime example. We read his story in John 5:2–6 (NASB):

> Now there is in Jerusalem by the sheep gate a pool, which is called in Hebrew Bethesda, having five porticoes. In these lay a multitude of those who were sick, blind, lame, and withered, waiting for the moving of the waters; for an angel of the Lord went down at certain seasons into the pool and stirred up the water; whoever then first, after the stirring up of the water, stepped in was made well from whatever disease with which he was afflicted. A man was there who had been ill for thirty-eight years. When Jesus saw him lying there, and knew that he had already been a long time in that condition, He said to him, "Do you wish to get well?"

If you've been victimized and suffered long-term or devastating consequences as a result, Jesus is asking you the same question, "Do you wish to get well? Do you want to be healed?" You won't receive your vindication with a victim mentality. The two simply do not mix. Jesus is ready to vindicate you, but you have to want the success more than the self-pity.

When I read John 5:7, I imagine the sick man speaking to Jesus in a whiney voice: "Sir, I have no man to put me into the pool when the water is stirred up, but while I am coming, another steps down before me" (NASB). Clearly, this man had a victim mentality. His answer should have been, "Yes, Lord," or even, "I believe; help my unbelief."

The lame man felt victimized because no one would help him get into the water. Here was this man sitting on the edge of a breakthrough yet unable to see the opportunity. He only saw the challenge. His victim mindset overshadowed any positive possibility.

If it were me and I knew an angel was coming to stir healing waters, I would have scooted myself to the edge of the pool. I would have devised a plan or paid someone to roll me over into the pool when the angel showed up. But instead of seeking a solution, the lame man had a lame attitude. He identified as a victim. The victim mentality had a stronghold in his soul

I mean, think about it. Instead of receiving his healing from the great physician standing right before him, he was whining to Jesus about why he couldn't get healed. His identity was wrapped up in his obstacles, trials, and warfare. He couldn't see through the victim-colored lenses.

Jesus didn't show him any pity. But He did show him compassion. John 5:8 shows how Jesus responded to his victim-laced complaint: "Get up, pick up your pallet and walk" (NASB). Scripture says immediately the man became well, picked up his pallet, and began to walk. Jesus wants to help you overcome the victim mentality. The first step is acknowledging you carry this mindset.

SIGNS OF A VICTIM MENTALITY

What is a victim mentality? Simply stated, a victim mentality is the mindset that convinces you that you are a victim. Henry Cloud, best-selling author of *Changes That*

Heal, says: "Victims declare, 'The world is responsible for me' and never do anything to better their quality of life."[1]

The truth is we aren't born with a victim mentality. We develop this mindset through suffering injustices, tragedies, or abuse. To be sure, there was a trigger event that started the victimhood cycle—a cycle you can and must break if you want to see vindication. You may not even realize you have a victim mentality—and that's part of the deception. If you could see it as a mindset that delays or even derails your vindication, you would immediately reject it.

If you'll keep your heart open, you may see yourself in one or more of these twelve signs of the victim mentality listed in this chapter. Pray before you read this next section and ask the Lord to expose any victim mentalities that are hindering your vindication.

1. You may have a victim mentality if you feel powerless to fix the problems in your life or even cope with them. Remember, the crippled man felt powerless to get into the water first. The truth is you are not powerless. The Spirit that raised Christ from the dead dwells in you (Rom. 8:11). That truth makes you powerful!

2. You may have a victim mentality if you magnify injustice and exalt the enemy's power over God's power. In other words, you concentrate on what the devil has done to the point that you're magnifying the destructive work of Satan instead of magnifying the restorative work of the Savior.

Psalm 34:3–5 tells us plainly, "Oh, magnify the Lord with me, and let us exalt His name together. I sought the Lord, and He heard me, and delivered me from all my fears." *Magnify* means "to increase in significance" or "to enlarge in fact or in appearance."[2] When we magnify the devil's facts over God's truth, we live as victims. When we magnify the Lord, we live as victors.

3. You may have a victim mentality if you think people are out to get you and even wonder sometimes if God is on your side. This may ultimately manifest as paranoia. We think of Romans 8:31, "If God is for me, who can be against me?" Sometimes we just don't understand why God would let the injustice happen.

I can imagine how Joshua felt after the massive slaughter against Ai. In Joshua 1:5, God told him clearly, "No man will be able to stand against you all the days of your life. As I was with Moses, I will be with you. I will not abandon you. I will not leave you" (MEV). But then Israel was defeated at Ai and Joshua wasted no time accusing God: "O Lord GOD, why did You bring this people across the Jordan to give us into the hands of the Amorites to destroy us?" (Josh. 7:7, MEV).

I understand why Joshua was confused. God said He would help him, and suddenly he lost a major battle. Did God lie? No, the enemy attacked. There was an open door, but Joshua didn't discern it. Achan had taken spoils from the last war, which God prohibited. Joshua didn't know it until the Lord exposed it. Thankfully, Joshua quickly shook off the victim mindset and rallied to win the next battle. So can you.

4. You may have a victim mentality if you get easily offended when someone tries to help you see your life from God's perspective, or you reject godly counsel because you feel like no one understands your plight. You

may justify your victim mentality with words like the bitter man I met at the gas station offered: "But you don't understand…" There is no justification for victimhood. For freedom's sake, Christ died to set you free (Gal. 5:1).

5. You may have a victim mentality if you refuse to take any responsibility for your position in life. You don't consider that you may be responding through the wrong lens to the circumstances in which you find yourself. You blame the devil, other people, and even God but don't look at how you contributed to your woes by disobeying God, failing to acknowledge Him in a big decision, or otherwise missing His warnings or instructions. Remember this, life is not fair, but God is just.

6. You may have a victim mentality if you get upset when people don't give you the sympathy you think you deserve. When they don't RSVP to your pity party, you feel rejected. The only ones who join in your pity party are other miserable people who want to take turns complaining about their lives.

7. You may have a victim mentality if you host your own private pity parties. Here's the deception: you think it's a private party, but self-pity attracts devils. Although the Holy Spirit won't attend your "woe is me" gathering, demons show up to celebrate your misery.

8. You may have a victim mentality if you walk in a state of fear, doubt, and negativity about your circumstances. Really listen to yourself talk, and you will hear what everyone else around you already knows by your speech. Remember, out of the abundance of your heart, your mouth speaks (Luke 6:45).

9. You may have a victim mentality if "I can't" is a

keyword in your vocabulary. And that's a lie. The truth is you can do all things through Christ who strengthens you (Phil. 4:13). The problem is, "I can't" often turns into "I don't want to" or even "I won't."

10. You may have a victim mentality if you feel like you have the right to complain about your circumstances or what "they" did to you. But consider this: Jesus never complained about what happened to Him, and He suffered much more than any of us ever will.

When the victim mindset matures, you regress. Eventually, you feel like you deserve what you are getting. That's the eleventh sign. The twelfth sign is outward-facing. If you are not careful, the victim mentality can drive you to take vengeance into your own hands. If you shed the victim mentality, healing and vindication begin.

DEVELOPING A MORE-THAN-A-CONQUEROR MENTALITY

The Bible calls us more than conquerors (Rom. 8:37). The Complete Jewish Bible uses the term "superconquerors." We need God's grace to step into those tights and put on that cape because the enemy's kryptonite is real.

When Moses sent the twelve Israelite spies into the Promised Land to have a look-see, ten of them came back with a victim mentality. The vision of the giant caused them to become "like grasshoppers in our own sight, and so we were in their sight" (Num. 13:33, NASB). When we take on the victim mentality, it draws more victimization into our lives.

Thankfully, Joshua and Caleb modeled the right mindset—the conquering mindset. "Then Caleb quieted the people before Moses, and said, "Let us go up at once and take possession, for we are well able to overcome it" (Num. 13:30). A generation of victim-minded Israelites died in the wilderness. But Joshua and Caleb entered the Promised Land.

Caleb never lost his conquering mindset. When it was time for him to claim his inheritance in the Promised Land, he was eighty-five years old. But he told Joshua, "As yet I am as strong this day as I was in the day that Moses sent me: as my strength was then, even so is my strength now, for war, both to go out, and to come in" (Josh. 14:11, KJV). And Caleb took the mountains despite the enemies in the land opposing him.

Developing a conquering mentality is a matter of perspective. Are you going to see yourself as victorious in Christ or a victim of the giants in the land? Will you see yourself as more than a conqueror or as a grasshopper? It's your choice—and only you can make it.

We overcome a victim mentality by developing faith in the Word of God, what it says about who we are in Christ, and what we can do in His strength. It may take time to renew your mind, but it's never too early to start. First John 5:4 puts it this way, "This is the victory that overcomes the world, even our faith" (KJV).

CHAPTER 7

CRYING OUT FOR VINDICATION

WHEN MY DAUGHTER was a newborn, her faintest cry would wake me up out of the deepest sleep. Her little whimper may as well have been an industrial siren alarm with strobe lights demanding my immediate attention. If you've ever had a baby, you know what I mean.

What's more, I could discern my baby's cry from any other baby's cry—and I could translate the meaning of each kind of cry. The "I'm hungry" cry was loud and insistent, while the "I'm colicky" cry was fussy and persistent. No matter the sound of the cry, I dropped everything I was doing and ran to ease her distress. I did this because she is my child, and I love her.

You are God's child, and He loves you. What's more, He never sleeps or slumbers. (See Psalm 121:4.) Rest assured, when you cry out for vindication, He hears you. And when you turn to Him instead of taking matters into your own hands, He delights in your prayer.

We need to get a revelation of the power of crying out to God—a revelation David understood and put into practice over and over again throughout the Book of

Psalms. Indeed, David used "crying out" as a weapon in his vindication toolbox again and again.

In Psalm 56:9, David writes, "When I cry out to You, then my enemies will turn back; this I know, because God is for me." And again, "I will cry out to God Most High, to God who performs all things for me" (Ps. 57:2). And again, "Then they cry out to the LORD in their trouble, and He brings them out of their distresses" (Ps. 107:28).

GOD HEARS YOUR CRIES

Many times, we cry over the painful events in our lives. We shed tears and wallow in self-pity over what someone did to us. There's no power in self-centered sobbing. Instead, we need to cry out to our vindicator. The Hebrew word translated "cry" in the psalms quoted previously isn't a pitiful lament; it's a powerful prayer that turns the tables on the enemy.

Strong's Concordance reveals that "cry" (*qārā'* in Hebrew) means to "utter a loud sound," "call (with name of God)," and "summon."[1] This desperate sound beckons God to vindicate you in the face of even the worst enemy attack. When you find people "crying out" and "crying aloud" to get God's attention in the pages of Scripture, they experience vindication.

While you may feel like God does not hear your desperate cries for vindication, He does. Just because you don't see an at-once answer to your cries doesn't mean God is not moving behind the scenes to deliver vindication. Your vindication will come to pass in God's appointed time. The Israelites were in bondage to Egyptian rule for four hundred years, but God eventually vindicated them. (Don't worry. You won't have to wait that long!)

Exodus 2:23–25: "Now it happened in the process of time that the king of Egypt died. Then the children of Israel groaned because of the bondage, and they cried out; and their cry came up to God because of the bondage. So God heard their groaning, and God remembered His covenant with Abraham, with Isaac, and with Jacob. And God looked upon the children of Israel, and God acknowledged them."

Catch that. The Israelites' cry came up to God because of the bondage—even though their own sin was what landed them in bondage. Their desperate cries touched God's heart and moved His hand. God's arm is not too short to deliver nor His ear too heavy to hear (Isa. 59:1). The Lord raised up Moses to deliver and vindicate His people.

No matter how long it takes, your part in the equation is not to vindicate yourself. Whatever measure of vindication you can work up for yourself is short-lived and less than satisfying. Your role is to cry out to your vindicator until His promises come to pass. That means you need to stand in faith as you cry out. That's what David did time and time again.

WHEN YOU MADE YOUR OWN MESS

Psalm 34:17 assures us, "The righteous cry out, and the LORD hears, and delivers them out of all their troubles." Again, even if you caused yourself trouble with a poor decision to engage in a toxic relationship, invest money in the wrong venture, or "fill in the blank," you can cry out in repentance—and then cry out for justice.

The Lord will take pity on you and deliver you when you repent. No matter what you have done to get yourself into a mess, God will not turn His back on you when you cry out. You can boldly approach His throne of grace to find help and obtain mercy in a time of need (Heb. 4:16). He's that good!

In the Book of Judges, we see Israel commit spiritual adultery and follow after other gods until the Lord allowed their enemies to conquer them. But in His mercy, when the Israelites cried out to the Lord in repentance, God always raised up a deliverer to vindicate them. The Israelites repeated this cycle of spiritual adultery and repentance, but God was nevertheless faithful to answer their desperate cries.

If we're honest, we often repeat foolish patterns in our lives. We make mistakes, don't notice the enemy creeping in, let our prayer life slack, or engage in sinful behaviors until we finally find ourselves in a miserable condition. But when we cry out in repentance, God will deliver us. And when we cry out, He will vindicate us. It may take time for God to work out all the circumstances you got yourself into, but the sound of your desperate cry will get God's attention, and He will move on your behalf.

Psalm 145:19 tells us, "He will fulfill the desire of those who fear Him; He also will hear their cry and save them." He hears your cries for breakthrough in the situation that's trying to break you. David knew this, which was why he often prayed along these lines: "Hear my cry, O God; attend to my prayer" (Ps. 61:1). And again, "Hear a just cause, O LORD, attend to my cry; give ear to my prayer which is not from deceitful lips" (Ps. 17:1).

RELEASING YOUR BATTLE CRY

Sometimes your crying out is an all-out battle cry against the enemy of your soul. The battle cry, then, becomes a shout for vindication. A shout is, by definition, loud! The Hebrew word for *shout—tsarach*—has several definitions, including "roar," "make a shrill or clear sound," and to cry out as in a battle cry.[2] There are times to release an aggressive, militant war cry in the battle for your vindication.

The Israelites stood trembling in silence when Goliath called for a soldier to stand toe-to-toe with them in the Valley of Elah. But when the Israelites heard the sound of Goliath hitting the ground and the Philistine army fleeing, they released a battle cry:

> Now the men of Israel and Judah arose and shouted, and pursued the Philistines as far as the entrance of the valley and to the gates of Ekron. And the wounded of the Philistines fell along the road to Shaaraim, even as far as Gath and Ekron. Then the children of Israel returned from chasing the Philistines, and they plundered their tents.
> —1 SAMUEL 17:52–53

The shout—the war cry—sent a clear message to the Philistines that Israel was no longer paralyzed with fear but mobilized in unity. I imagine the Philistines never forgot that day or the sound of an emboldened Israeli army pursuing them. When you release a shout, make sure it's loud enough to catch the enemy's attention and make him regret stirring the lion within you.

Long before David slayed the giant with a sling and a stone, Gideon led a small army into what looked like an impossible-to-win battle. Jehovah commissioned Gideon to deliver Israel from the cruel hands of the Midianites. Gideon could hardly believe his ears when God called him a "mighty man of valor" and sent him to set Israel free from captivity (Judg. 6:11). In fact, Gideon put out two fleeces to make doubly sure he was accurately hearing the Lord before he became the reluctant captain of His troops.

YOUR BATTLE CRY PANICS THE ENEMY

You know the story: God rooted out all Israelites who were fearful or who knelt to drink water. Gideon was left with only three hundred soldiers to fight against 135,000 Midianites (Judg. 7:16). Gideon was more than a little nervous at the prospect, but God, in His mercy, gave him a third and final prophetic sign.

Here's how it happened: Gideon overheard a Midianite telling his friend about a dream he had the night before. In the dream, a loaf of barley bread tumbled into the Midianite camp and struck a tent. The tent collapsed. The interpretation: "This is nothing else but the sword of Gideon the son of Joash, a man of Israel! Into his hand God has delivered Midian and the whole camp" (Judg. 7:14).

With this, Gideon was emboldened and addressed his small army. We see what happens next in Judges 7:15–20 (NLT):

When Gideon heard the dream and its interpretation, he bowed in worship before the LORD. Then he returned to the Israelite camp and shouted, "Get up! For the LORD has given you victory over the Midianite hordes!" He divided the 300 men into three groups and gave each man a ram's horn and a clay jar with a torch in it.

Then he said to them, "Keep your eyes on me. When I come to the edge of the camp, do just as I do. As soon as I and those with me blow the rams' horns, blow your horns, too, all around the entire camp, and shout, 'For the LORD and for Gideon!'"

It was just after midnight, after the changing of the guard, when Gideon and the 100 men with him reached the edge of the Midianite camp. Suddenly, they blew the rams' horns and broke their clay jars. Then all three groups blew their horns and broke their jars. They held the blazing torches in their left hands and the horns in their right hands, and they all shouted, "A sword for the LORD and for Gideon!"

Gideon released his war cry, which caused the Midianites to rush around in a panic, shouting as they ran to escape. The shout and the blowing of the ram's horns caused the Midianite warriors to fight against each other. The ones who didn't die in battle ran as fast and as far away from the battlefield as they could. A battle cry was the beginning of the successful war campaign. Your battle cry can send panic into the enemy's camp.

DON'T STOP CRYING OUT

Most of the time, crying out is not a one-and-done deal. You may have to cry out for a long time—and with consistency—before you see vindication. Look at the martyrs in the Book of Revelation:

> When He opened the fifth seal, I saw under the altar the souls of those who had been slain for the word of God and for the testimony which they held. And they cried with a loud voice, saying, "How long, O Lord, holy and true, until You judge and avenge our blood on those who dwell on the earth?" Then a white robe was given to each of them; and it was said to them that they should rest a little while longer, until both the number of their fellow servants and their brethren, who would be killed as they were, was completed.
>
> —REVELATION 6:9–11

Vindication will surely come. Sometimes we must keep crying out. Take Job as an example. He cried out and then cried some more. But he didn't get an immediate response: "If I cry out concerning wrong, I am not heard. If I cry aloud, there is no justice" (Job 19:7). Yet he didn't stop crying out. Job 30:20 tells us, "I cry out to You, but You do not answer me." For all his crying out, David at times felt the same was a Job: "O My God, I cry in the daytime, but You do not hear; and in the night season, and am not silent" (Ps. 22:2).

The key is, "I am not silent." Don't stop crying out. In the parable of the persistent widow, Jesus taught us that we should always pray and not lose heart. As Jesus told it, a widow wanted vengeance against her enemies but the king would not cooperate. Because she was persistent in crying out for vindication, he finally relented.

Jesus said, "And shall God not avenge His own elect who cry out day and night to Him, though He bears long with them? I tell you that He will avenge them speedily. Nevertheless, when the Son of Man comes, will He really find faith on the earth?" (Luke 18:7–8). Keep crying out for vindication in faith. You will see it!

CHAPTER 8

DECREEING YOUR VINDICATION

WE WERE IN a torrential Kansas City, Kansas, rainstorm, completing last-minute preparations for our first intercessor's retreat, when we got a call from a member of our church back home. Without so much as a hello, she breathlessly told us that Awakening House of Prayer was all over the news in Fort Lauderdale, Florida. My first thought was that miracles broke out in the church when I wasn't there. What faith I had!

Unfortunately, we weren't headlining the 5:00 p.m. news because someone was raised from the dead. We were the feature story because the back wall of our building collapsed. And just that fast, Awakening House of Prayer was homeless. Everything the church owned was locked up inside the building, including $100,000 of media, worship, and office equipment—and the fire marshal wouldn't allow us to retrieve it for safety reasons. We didn't know where to go or what to do.

Adding insult to injury, a few mean-spirited onlookers started attacking us when I posted the news on social media, hoping to connect with someone who could point us to a temporary space for our church services. It was venomous. They insisted our misfortune was God's wrath falling on the ministry. They pointed to Paul the apostle's words: "I suffer not a woman to teach" (1 Tim. 2:12, KJV).

God quickly proved them wrong. He made a temporary way out of no way. An art gallery let us hold our service in their space for one week, and we found a hotel conference space for the next few weeks. But then the well dried up. I couldn't find available space anywhere. As I was sitting before the Lord, He whispered these words to my heart: "There are some battles you need to send your intercessors in to fight. But there are some battles where you need to lead the charge. Right now, you need to lead the charge."

With that, on a severely sprained ankle, I began to pace back and forth, praying and making decrees in my living room. Suddenly these words came out of my mouth: "I decree we will have a new building contract by 8-18-2018." Then I went silent. I was shocked by the words that came out of my mouth. I didn't dare tell a soul because we'd been looking for a suitable facility for six years to no avail. How would we find one in just a few days? (I made this decree on August 10, 2018!)

That's when I heard the Lord say, "Look on Craigslist." Craigslist is an online classified website where you can find jobs, merchandise, and rent spaces. I had scanned their listings many times over the years and found nothing. Nevertheless, like Peter, who cast his net to the other side of the boat at Christ's command after coming up empty all night long, I obeyed the Lord.

Long story short, I found a new facility on Craigslist, and we signed the contract on 8-18-2018. And our new facility was about a hundred times better than the one that collapsed. Not only did we have a new and better building, but God also vindicated me from the mean-spirited Christians.

THE POWER OF A DECREE

Like me, there comes a time when you need to decree your vindication. The word *decree* has lost some of its power in our modern world. A quick scan of news headlines reveals the watering down that has taken place. Decrees of divorce are easy to get. Fiscal decrees are readily appealed by governments. Technology companies breach federal decrees at will.

A *decree* is "an order usually having the force of law," according to *Merriam-Webster*'s dictionary.[1] While it seems decrees don't always carry the weight in the natural realm they should, decrees based on God's Word or inspired by the Holy Spirit pack a heavy punch in the spirit realm.

Decrees are common in judicial systems around the world. But decrees are first found in the Word of God. Think about it for a minute. God decreed the world into existence. I'll say that again: God decreed the world into existence. You've probably heard that God spoke the world into existence. But what He spoke was a clear decree. You've read in Scripture how God spoke, "Let there be light" (Gen. 1:3). A more accurate translation of what God said was "Light be." He decreed light into existence.

God framed the world with His decree. Hebrews 11:3 tells us, "By faith we understand that the universe was framed by the word of God, so that things that are seen were not made out of things which are visible" (MEV). He decreed what was not seen, and it manifested according to His will. We can operate in decrees in the same way, according to His will.

DECREE A THING!

There's a time for every purpose under heaven (Eccles. 3:1). There's a time to pray and praise God for your vindication. There's a time to keep thanking Him while you wait. There's a time to wage war against the enemy of your decree. There's a time to be still and know He is God. But there's also a time to decree.

Job 22:28 tells us plainly, "Thou shalt also decree a thing, and it shall be established unto thee: and the light shall shine upon thy ways" (KJV). Different translations shed interesting light on this verse. For example, the New International Version tells us, "What you decide on will be done, and light will shine on your ways." The Contemporary English Version puts it this way: "He will do whatever you ask, and life will be bright."

The Amplified Bible, Classic Edition expounds on this truth a little more: "You shall also decide and decree a thing, and it shall be established for you; and the light [of God's favor] shall shine upon your ways." *The Message* assures, "You'll decide what you want, and it will happen; your life will be bathed in light."

If you embrace this word—and by embrace, I don't mean just saying "yes and amen"; I mean taking faith-inspired action—you'll see radical change in time. You may see God bring vindication through opening the windows of heaven, reconciling broken relationships, healing your body, promoting you in your career, and more. Remember, when the enemy is caught stealing, he must repay seven times (Prov. 6:31).

YOUR ROYAL PRIESTHOOD

You are both priest and king. From the world's perspective—and even from a Hebraic perspective—the roles of king and priest are strikingly different. The office of the king and priest represent two distinct functions. A king doesn't offer sacrifices, and a priest does not rule. In the New Testament, however, Christians are both kings and priests. Revelation 1:6 says He has made us "kings and priests to His God and Father."

Most believers are comfortable with the priestly anointing to petition God in prayer for a thing but have not embraced the kingly anointing to decree a thing and see it established. To be sure, the concept of our priesthood has been etched in many believers' minds. First Peter 2:9 tells us, "But you are a chosen race, a royal priesthood, a holy nation, a people for God's own possession, so that you may declare the goodness of Him who has called you out of darkness into His marvelous light" (MEV).

But "royal priesthood" indicates a race of kings and priests. Kings don't put out petitions. Kings make decrees. As kings, we can decree the Word of God or the revealed will of God through prophecy. There is power in the Word of God. Heaven and earth will pass away, but His Word will never pass away (Matt. 24:35). His Word is life to all those who find them and healing to the flesh (Prov. 4:22).

God's Word will add length to your life and give you peace (Prov. 3:2). The grass withers and the flowers fade away, but the Word of God will stand forever (Isa. 40:8). His Word is spirit and life (John 6:63). His Word is truth (John 17:17). His Word is pure, like silver tried in a furnace, purified seven times (Ps. 12:6).

God expects us to follow His decrees. (See Leviticus 18:4.) But the enemy is also bound to obey a prophetic declaration in the name of Jesus, the name at which every knee must bow and every tongue confess that He is Lord (Rom. 14:11). Decrees establish the will of the Lord. Decrees shift circumstances. Decrees activate angels on assignment. Decrees can unlock your vindication. Decrees release divine judgment against the enemy and his plans for your life.

You may have made mistakes. You may even have fallen into sin. But when we truly repent, we can decree Romans 8:28 over our life: "We know that all things work together for good to those who love God, to those who are called according to His purpose" (MEV). Remember, your vindication does not rest on your blamelessness. It rests on God's faithfulness.

CHAPTER 9

SECRET SLANDER EXPOSED

I SAW THE DEVIL's digital dossier. I saw my name and mug shot splashed across the screen. I saw a highly organized document ticking down a laundry list of defamations.

Topping the list, I saw juvenile jabs criticizing me for the brand of coffee I drink, my mannerisms, and the pitch of my voice. Slanderous words from betrayers were next in line. These twisted truths were whispered behind closed doors before going viral, infecting one person after another until a false perception of who I am was forged in the minds of people who dine on gossip. Moving further down the malicious menu were severe slander accounts that sought to destroy my good name.

I saw all this in a dream that exposed the enemy's defamation strategy against me. Indeed, the Holy Spirit was showing me things to come so I could prepare my heart for future assaults. Unfortunately, all the prayers in the world didn't stop some of the slander—but God has vindicated me from every attack. To this day, people come up and apologize to my face for what they believed about me behind my back.

The Puritans used to say, "The devil was first a slanderer and liar, and then a murderer, John 8:44. He cannot murder without the slander first....A malicious heart and a slanderous tongue always go well together."[1]

SEEING THE SLANDER

Slander is not pretty. It means "to defame someone; to harm their reputation; to disgrace; or to accuse." Consider this: the word translated "slanderer" in 1 Timothy 3:11 is the same word translated "devil." When someone slanders us, they are acting like devils. They are mirroring the character of Satan. We can't respond in kind. We can't walk in the anointing God has for us and mirror the character of Satan at the same time. We just can't.

I've experienced seasons of what I call "slander floods," usually from atheists or radicals who oppose the truth I am sharing. When the slander comes in like a flood, know this: you're doing something right. Jesus said we'd be lied about just as He was lied about.

No one likes to be slandered. I don't enjoy it. But it makes me sorrowful for the one who's sinning. The Bible says, "Whoever secretly slanders his neighbor, Him I will destroy" (Ps. 101:5). And Romans 1:30–32 suggests backbiters are worthy of death. Paul told us not to keep company with a believer who has "a foul tongue [railing, abusing, reviling, slandering]" (1 Cor. 5:11, AMPC). Scripture lists the slanderer among the sexually immoral, the covetous, idolaters, drunkards and extortioners. The point is, God hates slander.

Understanding how seriously God takes slander has had a twofold impact on my heart. First, I don't want any part of slander. I don't want to engage in it, and I won't listen to anyone else spewing it. If someone comes to me with slander on their lips, I put out the fire and bring gentle correction to help them avoid Satan's snare. Second, when I see the damage the slanderer is doing to himself by attacking me, I take pity on them. While they think their words are digging a pit for me, they are the ones who are bound to fall headlong into the hole.

RESPONDING TO SLANDER

How you respond to mistreatment is one of the most critical aspects of your spiritual life. When we respond the right way, we climb higher—or go deeper—in the Spirit. In fact, a season of slander is a sure sign that you are up for a promotion.

Paul told Timothy: "Indeed, all who delight in pursuing righteousness and are determined to live godly lives in Christ Jesus will be hunted and persecuted [because of their faith]" (2 Tim. 3:12, AMP). Oftentimes, slander is part of that persecution. We have to see slander as a stepping stone to greater success.

I've endured plenty of mistreatment during my life, and I can honestly say that I count it a blessing. By God's grace, I've managed to respond in meekness rather than retaliating against the poor soul manifesting the character of slanderous Satan. And I pray that God's grace will continue to pour over me as the slander from religious spirits, atheists, radical activists, and occasionally even those who I let get close to me who have believed the enemy's lie continues.

By contrast, when we respond the wrong way, we get

bitter. Over time, that bitterness will defile our spirits and dull our ability to sense the presence of God or hear His voice. Bitterness is deadly—and it's easy for the people around you to discern. Where true humility lives, though, bitterness can't take up residence. But I'm getting ahead of myself.

DYING TO YOUR OWN REPUTATION

I've learned over the years to transfer my personal rights to God, knowing He will vindicate me amid the slander—or any other mistreatment. And He has confirmed me time and time again in the presence of my enemies when I give Him the reins. As Paul wrote, "You were bought with a price. Therefore glorify God in your body and in your spirit, which are God's" (1 Cor. 6:20, MEV). I've committed my spirit into the Lord's hands, and in return, He takes responsibility for my protection, provision, and vindication when necessary.

I don't want to be like the accuser of the brethren. And I don't want to swap insult for insult (1 Pet. 3:9). I want to be like Jesus, who, "when He was reviled, He did not revile back; when He suffered, He did not threaten, but He entrusted Himself to Him who judges righteously" (1 Pet. 2:23, MEV).

God is the judge. He will make the wrong things right in His way and in His timing. Vengeance is His; He will repay (Rom. 12:19). I won't be overcome with evil, but I will overcome evil with good (v. 21). I will rejoice when I am persecuted because I know that when I respond the right way, I am blessed. My first response is to pray for those who persecute me. And pray. And pray some more. It keeps my heart clean. I encourage you to do the same.

The initial sting fades more quickly when you walk in love, speak the truth in love without being defensive, and refuse to retaliate. I've also found it true that God repays, vindicates, and takes vengeance on my behalf. You can have the same testimony if you respond with meekness in the face of mistreatment.

OVERCOME EVIL WITH GOOD

Back to my dream about the digital dossier. My first response was to pray against the slander manifesting. These slanderous words were like bullets in the enemy's gun. Some of them he had already fired. I feel confident the slander I did not see were bullets the enemy has not yet released. So I bind the accusations, and I examine my heart to make sure I am walking circumspectly and worthy of my calling so I can claim 1 Peter 3:17, "For it is better to suffer [unjustly] for doing right, if that should be God's will, than [to suffer justly] for doing wrong" (AMP).

Take to heart what Christ said in Matthew 5:11–12 (AMPC):

> Blessed (happy, to be envied, and spiritually prosperous—with life-joy and satisfaction in God's favor and salvation, regardless of your outward conditions) are you when people revile you and persecute you and say all kinds of evil things against you falsely on My account. Be glad and supremely joyful, for your reward in heaven is great (strong and intense), for in this same way people persecuted the prophets who were before you.

CHAPTER 10

SURVIVING THE STING
OF BETRAYAL

I TREATED HIM LIKE a son. He saw me as a spiritual mother. He even called me Mom—until the day he conspired with another "son" to put a knife in my back. And I never saw it coming.

Rafael was a bright and shining star, and he was like a sponge. Several years my junior, Rafael soaked up all the wisdom I could pour out and applied it to his life and budding ministry. He was the model son. As the relationship progressed, he asked me to train him at a deeper level.

Rafael started talking with me about moving to South Florida with his family and serving for a year at the ministry I founded, Awakening House of Prayer, to learn about planting and building a church. He would shadow me in ministry and glean from how we stewarded the anointing, handled church conflicts, and received and executed divine strategies. After a year, Rafael would plant a church. At least, that was the plan.

But soon the other "son," Mark, got in Rafael's head. Mark didn't want Rafael to move to South Florida because he was helping him build his ministry elsewhere.

Rather than coming into agreement with God's plan for Rafael, Mark secretly convinced him to skip the year of training and plant a church immediately. Mark even vowed to help him.

It happened so fast my head was spinning. The two sons essentially divorced me as "mom" and collaborated on their ministries together—covertly tapping into my ministry staff to do so. I was shocked when I found out people from my ministry were sowing into these way-ward sons because they thought it would bless and honor me. They had no idea these sons had become Judas and Absalom.

It took time to unravel the deception behind this betrayal—or, I should say, double betrayal. It was a blindside, or what the dictionary calls a *coup*—"a brilliant, sudden, and usually highly successful stroke or act."[1] The plot was exposed without my voicing a word. After I pulled the knives out of my back, I did the only thing I could do: forgive and believe God for double vindication.

JESUS GETS IT

As one who studied Latin for three years in high school, I learned how Brutus betrayed Roman dictator Julius Caesar. Brutus was the ruler's close friend, yet took part in a coup to assassinate him. When Julius recognized Brutus as one of the assailing parties, he exclaimed the now famous words, "Et tu Brute?" which means, "You too, Brutus?"

Well, at least that's the accent of the historical event from Shakespeare. The British playwright may have been drawing some imagery from the life of Jesus, as

Christ faced a similar episode. Luke 22 gives the familiar account of Judas' midnight betrayal, but don't gloss over this Garden of Gethsemane event too quickly or you'll miss the point.

Matthew's Gospel puts it this way: "While he was still speaking, Judas, one of the Twelve, arrived. With him was a large crowd armed with swords and clubs, sent from the chief priests and the elders of the people. Now the betrayer had arranged a signal with them: 'The one I kiss is the man; arrest him.' Going at once to Jesus, Judas said, 'Greetings, Rabbi!' and kissed him. Jesus replied, 'Do what you came for, friend'" (Matt. 26:47–50, NIV). Luke offered this insight: "Jesus said to him, 'Judas, are you betraying the Son of Man with a kiss?'" (Luke 22:48, NIV).

The difference between Jesus and Julius (and most of us) is Jesus saw the betrayal coming. Most of us do not. But notice how both betrayals came from "friends." You can expand "friends" to include business partners, coworkers, employers, pastors, spiritual sons and daughters, and so on. Betrayal takes on many different faces, but it always has the same treacherous agenda. In any case, when you are betrayed, Jesus understands your pain.

WHY, GOD, WHY?

All relationships come with a betrayal risk. Studies show most of the betrayals we experience come from close friends (27 percent) or romantic partners (30 percent). Other betrayals involve family members and people in the workplace. That about covers every area of life![2]

I have found myself in betrayal situations in all four categories. Sometimes people betray you because their motives were never right to begin with—and you didn't pick up on it because you chose to believe the best or just flat-out missed the Holy Spirit's warning.

Other times, betrayal arises because people change. Some people start with the best intentions toward you, but over time, the enemy turns them against you through misunderstandings, jealousy, or false accusations. Still other times, people think they can't trust you and decide to betray you before you betray them.

Indeed, there are many reasons why people betray you. Disappointment seems to be a primary motivator. Judas betrayed Jesus because He didn't plan to take kingship in the natural realm to free Israel from Roman rule. When people expect you to be something you are not, their disappointment may lead them to destroy you.

Ungodly ambitions will also drive people to betray you. I've had people use me to get an open door, but as soon as I opened the door, they slammed it shut in my face. Greed is another common denominator in many betrayals. Some people will do just about anything for money, including selling out a close friend to make a lucrative business deal.

In whatever way it comes, betrayal is usually wrapped in the deception of justification. Betrayers feel justified in their wicked works of darkness. I've said this in the past, but it bears repeating: people outside your inner circle will persecute and malign you, but they can't truly betray you because betrayal implies trust that has been broken.

RESPONDING TO BETRAYAL

You may be in a season when everywhere you look, someone you thought you could trust betrays you; someone you thought had your back stabbed you in the back; someone you were closely aligned with allied with someone who openly opposes you.

So how do you respond when people to whom you have been friendly, helpful, and loyal betray your trust? You'll probably get hurt, mad, and then really mad. You'll probably relate to David in Psalm 41:9, "Even my best friend, the one I always told everything—he ate meals at my house all the time!—has bitten my hand" (MSG).

If you've been betrayed, you have to forgive. But if you are surrounded by would-be Judases—those you discern may be working against you—you have to walk in love and embrace Psalm 37. I had to learn to do this in the midst of what I call a Judas trial. The Holy Spirit told me, "Trust in the LORD, and do good" (v. 3, MEV). Listen in to some of the rest of this psalm and let it encourage your heart:

> Do not fret because of evildoers, nor be jealous of those who do injustice. For they will quickly wither like the grass, and fade like the green herbs. Trust in the LORD, and do good; dwell in the land, and practice faithfulness. Delight yourself in the LORD, and He will give you the desires of your heart.
>
> Commit your way to the LORD; trust also in Him, and He will bring it to pass. He will bring forth your righteousness as the light, and your judgment as the noonday. Rest in the LORD, and

> wait patiently for Him; do not fret because of those who prosper in their way, because of those who make wicked schemes. Let go of anger, and forsake wrath; do not fret—it surely leads to evil deeds. For evildoers will be cut off, but those who hope in the Lord will inherit the earth.
>
> —Psalm 37:1–9, mev

YOU HAVE A CHOICE

When you are betrayed, you have two choices: You can sink to your hater's level and enjoy the temporary satisfaction of attacking them in the same spirit in which they attacked you, or you can decide to move in the opposite spirit—the Spirit of Christ—and allow Him to prepare a table before you in the presence of your enemies (Ps. 23:5).

Here's some wise advice: If betrayers strike out at you, don't try to defend yourself. Don't try to make people understand your side of the story. Don't engage in conversation with other people about the betrayal. It doesn't matter what people think. It matters what God thinks. And if God wants to show them the truth, He will do it. Trust God. When you refuse to retaliate, God will vindicate! Whether you see that vindication immediately or it takes years, hold on to these words from Romans 8:33–37:

> Who shall bring a charge against God's elect? It is God who justifies. Who is he who condemns? It is Christ who died, and furthermore is also risen, who is even at the right hand of God, who also makes intercession for us. Who shall separate us from the love of Christ? Shall tribulation, or distress, or persecution, or famine, or nakedness, or

peril, or sword? As it is written: "For Your sake we are killed all day long; we are accounted as sheep for the slaughter." Yet in all these things we are more than conquerors through Him who loved us.

Amen.

I don't know about you, but that changes everything for me. God is our vindicator. We can't always trust people, but we can certainly always trust Him. Keep in mind the words of Charles Spurgeon, known in the 1800s as the "prince of preachers": "Every reputation that has been obscured by the clouds of reproach, for Christ's sake, shall be rendered glorious."[3]

CHAPTER 11

WHEN LIFE'S NOT FAIR

IT WAS A classic bait and switch, and it was a "Christian" marketing firm that set it up! This firm advertised "unlimited," top-quality graphic design work for a flat monthly fee. The way I saw it, I was being a good steward. This would save our ministry donor dollars. The firm showed me stellar samples of their work and presented endorsements from megachurches. It seemed like an obvious decision.

After I signed a contract with them, I sent in my first graphic request. That's when the firm shared its "throttle" policy. As it turned out, the service wasn't really "unlimited." The company would only produce one graphic at a time with a three-day turnaround time, so customers received a maximum of ten graphics a month. That's hardly unlimited. Adding insult to injury, the quality was nothing like the portfolio displayed on the firm's website. I saw this as an unethical business practice. It wasn't fair!

After week one, I had received only one graphic—and it looked like a five-year-old created it. Since the company offered a money-back guarantee, I asked for a refund. My request was sharply refused. Moreover, the "Christian" CEO texted me insisting no one had ever been successful

in winning a credit card dispute against his company—
and threatened to sue me if I dared to try.

Talk about going on the offensive! I hadn't even suggested disputing the charge. I just asked them to make
good on their refund policy. By this time, I was a pro at
believing God in the face of injustice. I prayed, and God
told me, "Put it in My hands." I did, and He immediately
vindicated me. The money was swiftly returned.

LIFE IS NOT FAIR, BUT GOD IS JUST

God is not only just, but He's also incapable of injustice.
Believe me, the injustices you suffer do not go unnoticed
in heaven. But if you want vindication from injustice, you
need to believe God is a God of justice. Isaiah 30:18 tells
us plainly that the Lord is a God of justice, and when we
wait on Him, we're blessed. We may have to wait for justice to be served, but when divine justice comes, it's worth
waiting for.

The Lord loves justice (Ps. 33:5). Solomon contributed
this truth: Those who seek the Lord understand justice
completely (Prov. 28:5). Hear me well. The foundation
of God's throne is righteousness and justice (Ps. 89:14).
All His ways are justice (Deut. 32:4). God never perverts
justice (Job 8:3). In fact, He executes justice for the needy
(Ps. 140:12).

At the same time, God hates injustice. Solomon warned
that whoever sows injustice will reap calamity (Prov. 22:8).
Paul the apostle also understood this. He told his spiritual son Timothy, "Alexander the coppersmith did me
much harm. May the Lord repay him according to his
works" (2 Tim. 4:14). In fact, theologians say this is the

same Alexander whom Paul "delivered over to Satan that [he] may learn not to blaspheme" (1 Tim. 1:20).

What injustice did Alexander do to Paul? *John Gill's Exposition of the Bible* supposes, "It was very likely he had lately been at Rome, though now returned to Ephesus, and had done great injury to the apostle's character, and had reproached and reviled him as a man of bad principles and practices; his business is mentioned, to distinguish him from any other of that name, and to show the insolence of the man, that though he was an illiterate person, and in such a mean station of life, yet took upon him to resist the apostle and his doctrine."[1]

Whatever Alexander did, Paul was convinced the Lord would vindicate him. And whatever injustice you have suffered, God will vindicate you too. Your part is to forgive, bless, and ask the Lord for justice. And according to the example in Scripture, this is not a onetime event. You'll have to keep on asking until you see the vindication God wants to bring you.

DAVID ASKED FOR JUSTICE

David faced injustice over and over again throughout his lifetime. His father, Jesse, didn't even bother to call the ruddy boy out from the fields when Samuel came to anoint the next king. Later, a jealous King Saul tried to kill David, not once but many times. In a failed coup, David's son Absalom attempted to steal the kingdom right out from under his nose.

David cried out, "Vindicate me, O God, and plead my cause against an ungodly nation; oh, deliver me from the deceitful and unjust man!" (Ps. 43:1). When you face injustice, do what David did. Pray and know that God hears your cries. Exodus 22:23–24 confirms this, "If you afflict them in any way, and they cry at all to Me, I will surely hear their cry; and My wrath will become hot, and I will kill you with the sword."

God is not likely to kill your enemies, but they will reap what they sow if they don't repent. In other words, they will reap injustice. It's not a curse. It's a fact. God is not mocked; whatever a man sows, he will reap if he doesn't repent (Gal. 6:7). Sometimes even when the worker of injustice repents, there are still consequences. But remember, you are not the judge. You need to stand with a heart posture of blessing and mercy toward them.

Micah 6:8 offers this instruction from the Lord: "He has shown you, O man, what is good; and what does the LORD require of you but to do justly, to love mercy, and to walk humbly with your God?" Ask God for justice in humility and with persistence. But pray for God to have mercy on the one who did you wrong so you don't become like them.

THE UNJUST JUDGE

You are probably familiar with the parable of the persistent widow, but it's worth meditating on in this context. As you read Luke 18:1–7 (TLB), ask the Holy Spirit to give you a fresh revelation of its meaning:

> One day Jesus told his disciples a story to illustrate their need for constant prayer and to show them that they must keep praying until the answer comes. "There was a city judge," he said, "a very

godless man who had great contempt for everyone. A widow of that city came to him frequently to appeal for justice against a man who had harmed her. The judge ignored her for a while, but eventually she got on his nerves. 'I fear neither God nor man,' he said to himself, 'but this woman bothers me. I'm going to see that she gets justice, for she is wearing me out with her constant coming!'"

Then the Lord said, "If even an evil judge can be worn down like that, don't you think that God will surely give justice to his people who plead with him day and night?"

We're not pleading with God because He doesn't want to give us justice. The unjust judge does not represent God but is in contrast to God. The point of the parable is that if an unjust judge will deal with injustice, how much more swiftly will our just God vindicate us when we meet His conditions? His conditions, again, are to forgive, bless, and pray from a merciful heart posture.

When an injustice occurs, we want to be vindicated. "People feel that if they forgive the person who hurt them, then they will continue to take advantage of them or not take responsibility for what they did wrong," said Joyce Meyer, who was sexually abused by her father for over a decade.

"If we're honest, we'll admit that we usually want the person who hurt us to pay for what they did. We can't get past this until we get the revelation that only God can pay us back. He is our Vindicator and will heal and restore us if we will trust Him and forgive our enemies as He has told us to do."[2] Amen!

CHAPTER 12

THE ENEMY'S SMOKE AND MIRRORS

GALILEO REVOLUTIONIZED OUR understanding of the world. The Italian scientist and engineer, who lived from 1564 to 1642, supported the work of Copernicus, who claimed the earth revolved around the sun. The popular notion in his day was that the sun revolved around the earth. Not only were Galileo's theories controversial, but he was also considered a heretic!

Galileo was in good company. Abraham Lincoln was labeled a radical who would destroy the way of life for Southerners. Joan of Arc, who inspired a French revolt against the occupation of the English based on her divine visions, was accused of witchcraft and heresy. She was burned at the stake. Ralph Waldo Emerson once said, "To be great is to be misunderstood."[1]

I'm no Joan of Arc, but I know the pain of being misunderstood. I've been misunderstood my whole life. As a child, I was extremely shy—so shy, in fact, that people accused me of being a snob—and I had few friends. Fast-forward to my early twenties, and I entered the "grunge" phase. I dyed my hair blue, wore all black, and had one of my eyebrows pierced. That, of course, led to more misunderstandings—and the wrong friends.

Of course, that was nothing compared to what I would deal with in Christian media. I was attacked, maligned, and otherwise misunderstood with nearly every column I wrote during my eight years working as an editor at *Charisma* magazine. Atheists, witches—and even Christians with opposing views—twisted my words daily.

At first, I wanted to fight back. I carried a philosophy credited to Mark Twain, famed author of *Huckleberry Finn*, "Never argue with someone who buys ink by the barrel." Of course, answering my detractors just added fuel to the already raging fire. Over time, I developed skin like a rhinoceros—thick! Still, nobody likes to be misunderstood.

NAVIGATING MISUNDERSTANDINGS

Looking back, I can see the more influence God gave me, the more I was misunderstood. Indeed, the enemy fashioned misunderstanding as quasi-nuclear weapons against me. One of the most harrowing attacks was when another leader in the body of Christ was convinced I stole his book idea—because someone told him I did! His wife sent me a curt email that was nothing short of a cease-and-desist letter!

When I read the email, I broke out in a cold sweat and got sick to my stomach. First, I had not and would never steal anyone's book idea. Second, this man of God was so influential that he could have crushed me with his pinky. My intercessors stormed the gates of hell behind the scenes for days, but the misunderstanding was stubborn.

Out of desperation, I called an elder for some advice. This elder called the man of God who was believing the absolute worst about me and set the record straight.

It was all a misunderstanding—it was a demonic smoke and mirror strategy in which the truth was twisted by someone who didn't have enough integrity to check the facts before sharing information. Yes, I was writing a book on the same broad topic, but I had no idea this Christian leader had a similar book idea. Thankfully, the man of God saw the truth and later even called me to apologize—and helped me promote my book. That is God's vindication!

You can surely relate whether you're operating in full-time ministry or motherhood or everyday life. Nobody likes to be misunderstood. Indeed, it can be downright discouraging to do your utmost for His highest and have your own family, friends, and brothers and sisters in Christ misjudge your message and motives. So what's the vindication strategy? Let's take a close look at Joseph's story.

EXPLORING JOSEPH'S VINDICATION STRATEGY

Joseph could understand dreams, but it seems nobody could understand him. His family misunderstood his motives, but he didn't do himself any favors by sharing his divine dreams about the high call of God on his life. (See Genesis 37:4–10.) Family members rarely understand our calling unless they are on fire for the Lord themselves. Remember, Jesus said a prophet is not without honor except in his hometown (Mark 6:4). Joseph was so misunderstood that his brothers wanted to kill him.

89

How did Joseph handle this? He kept doing the right thing even when the wrong thing was happening to him. (Read that again!) I believe he carried that pain with him for the thirteen years it took him to get from the pit to the palace. When his brothers came to Egypt and he finally revealed himself to them, he wept. That may have been when all those hurts and wounds he carried deep in his heart came gushing out.

When we feel misunderstood or rejected, we may need to take a page out of Joseph's playbook and have a good cry. Let the pain out and ask God to take it away, heal our hearts, and help us forgive those who misunderstood us. That's what I have done—more than once.

One of the most painful misunderstandings I endured was at the hands of a pioneering couple I supported in ministry. For many years, they sang my praises and showed me great favor. When they moved into a new phase in life, they put me on the board of their new ministry. You might say they gave me a coat of many colors like Joseph.

This pioneering couple also made me the executor of their will and left me with a huge inheritance. We walked together for years until one day, the wife saw some ads on my blog that offended her. She asked me to remove them. I was happy to oblige. The challenge was I could not see what she was seeing. The ads she described were not anywhere on my blog. I asked my webmaster to check into it, and he could not see the ads either. This was another example of the enemy's smoke and mirror strategy.

Trying to solve the issue, we put the strictest filters on the ad server and hoped that would be the end of it. The wife apologized and thanked me for taking the ads down. Lo and behold, she saw similar ads a few days later. That was the straw that broke the camel's back—and broke the back of a ten-year relationship. She then attacked me and my character viciously. She disinherited me, took me off her board, and said many unkind things about me. I was shocked—and my heart was wounded.

I tried over the years to reconcile the relationship to no avail. When I found out her husband passed away, I wrote her a letter offering my deepest condolences. That's when she apologized for the misunderstanding with the blog and the hurt she caused me. That was God's vindication. When I read her letter, I cried like Joseph—and all that pain of misunderstanding came out.

JOB MASTERED MISUNDERSTANDINGS

If anyone was misunderstood, it was Job. His friends worked night and day to convince him he needed to repent of hidden sin. He was falsely accused. He was wrongly judged. On top of everything else, he suffered horribly from a series of severe circumstances the enemy brought his way.

What did Job do in response? The man of God had two strategies: First, he humbled himself under the mighty hand of God. Job cried out to God to show Him the error of His ways. Job 6:24 says, "Teach me, and I will hold my tongue; cause me to understand wherein I have erred." Second, Job kept on trusting God even when matters grew worse. His wife said, "Curse God and die" (Job 2:9)—but he refused.

But it wasn't until Job executed God's strategy that he

saw double for his trouble. It wasn't until Job prayed for his friends—the ones who added to his suffering through misunderstanding his heart—that he got his victory. Did you catch that? Part of your vindication strategy is praying for the ones who misunderstood you—and not praying they would get a revelation of how they are wrong but that God would bless them. When we do this, many times, the first thing God blesses them with is a revelation of how they misunderstood us.

HANNAH CONFRONTS MISUNDERSTANDING

And let's not forget Hannah. She was sorely misunderstood and falsely accused. There she was, pouring her heart out to God over her barrenness. Scripture says, "She was in bitterness of soul, and prayed to the LORD and wept in anguish" (1 Sam. 1:10). Then she made a vow to commit her child to the Lord if He would break the curse on her womb.

"And it happened, as she continued praying before the LORD, that Eli watched her mouth. Now Hannah spoke in her heart; only her lips moved, but her voice was not heard. Therefore Eli thought she was drunk. So Eli said to her, 'How long will you be drunk? Put your wine away from you!'" (vv.12–13). This, again, was the enemy's smoke and mirror strategy.

Hannah had three choices. She could have walked away angry, speaking ill of the priest, and becoming bitter and unforgiving. She could have walked away in misery, feeling sorry for herself, and accusing God. Or she could confront it respectfully.

She chose the latter and turned an accusation into a blessing:

> Hannah answered and said, "No, my lord, I am a woman of sorrowful spirit. I have drunk neither wine nor intoxicating drink, but have poured out my soul before the LORD. Do not consider your maidservant a wicked woman, for out of the abundance of my complaint and grief I have spoken until now." Then Eli answered and said, "Go in peace, and the God of Israel grant your petition which you have asked of Him."
>
> —1 SAMUEL 1:15–17

It's OK to confront misunderstandings in the right spirit.

MARY TRUSTED GOD TO CLEAR THE MATTER

Mary was about to marry Joseph when suddenly God called her to be the mother of the Messiah. When she found herself pregnant, she had no choice but to tell Joseph about her encounter with the angel Gabriel and to hope he would understand. It took great courage for Mary to tell him what surely sounded like an unbelievable story: "The Holy Ghost did it."

Understandably, Joseph had a hard time believing this. His emotions may have ranged from brokenhearted to angry over a perceived betrayal. Mary may have battled with fear and the pain of being misunderstood. After all, what woman wants the reputation of a harlot? According to Jewish law, if your fiancée turned up pregnant, you could either divorce her or have her stoned. (See Matthew 1:18–24.)

How did Mary handle the predicament? She had only one strategy: she trusted God. And God gave Joseph a dream and vindicated Mary.

Trusting God when you are misunderstood is often the only path to vindication. While you may be able to clarify simple misunderstandings with an honest conversation, speaking up to explain is no guarantee that you will be understood. Many times, as was the case with Job, trying to defend yourself only makes matters worse. You can never go wrong simply trusting God and following His lead.

GET OVER YOUR "SELF"

Sometimes we just need to get over our "self." The "misunderstood syndrome," as I call it, taps into self. It's our "self" that needs to feel understood. It's our "self" that feels rejected. It's our "self" that feels lonely. It's our "self" that gets depressed and wants to have a pity party.

When we feel misunderstood, we need to get our minds off ourselves and on somebody else. In other words, we need to get out there and help others who are in much worse positions than we are. It's amazing how the burdens lift when you get your mind off yourself. And while you are helping someone else, your vindicator will help you.

Ultimately, when people misunderstand us, they are not trying to hurt us. It's a misunderstanding. There's no sense in getting angry, resentful, bitter, or unforgiving over a misunderstanding—even if it leads to a painful accusation. Maybe they just can't understand because they haven't been in that place. But Jesus has.

Jesus was misunderstood—and it didn't bother His

self-esteem one bit. Most people didn't understand who Jesus was or what His mission was. Even those closest to Him—His family and His friends—did not understand Him. His family thought He was off His rocker. (See Mark 3:20–21.) Before the cross, He was an embarrassment to His brethren. He was even accused of being demon-possessed (Matt. 12:22–30).

How did Jesus respond to all of this? He spoke the truth in love and kept on going. He persevered on His mission and didn't give it another thought. His "nevertheless" attitude sought to do the will of God. Ultimately, millions would come to understand Him, but many more still do not.

Because Jesus was misunderstood, He understands how you feel when you are misunderstood. Take comfort knowing Jesus understands you perfectly (Heb. 4:15). He understands how you feel when people misinterpret your words or intentions. He understands how you feel when someone misjudges your character.

Jesus is a High Priest who understands—and His understanding is inexhaustible and boundless (Ps. 147:5). He is able immediately to run to the cry of those who are suffering (Heb. 2:18). These Scriptures will help you stay steady amid the pain of misunderstanding and the persecution that sometimes goes along with it.

GET YOUR MIND OFF THE MISUNDERSTANDING

Whether we face an honest misunderstanding or a nasty accusation, we need to respond rightly because the Lord is watching. He wants to vindicate us. So if you are misunderstood, here are some practical tips for getting your mind off the misunderstanding.

First, pray for those who misunderstood you. Next, be kind and respectful toward those who slight you. Seek the good of those who judge you wrongly. Protect the reputation of those who slander you. Privately work in the best interests of those who are working against you, and purposely avoid telling them what you do for them. Thank the Lord for the purifying effect it has on your life when you are misunderstood.

When we do these things, we have the Spirit of Jesus, "who, when He was reviled, did not revile in return; when He suffered, He did not threaten, but committed Himself to Him who judges righteously" (1 Pet. 2:23).

CHAPTER 13

WHEN THE THIEF COMES

COULD FEEL ENEMY resistance when I was writing *Developing Faith for the Working of Miracles*—a book based on a deep revelation that all things are possible to the one who believes. That's no great surprise since the enemy hates to see God glorified. But I wasn't expecting what happened next. It was an absolute blindside—and an absolute nightmare!

Just as I was putting the finishing touches on the book's final draft, the hard drive on my brand spanking new Mac computer failed. Devastated is not a strong enough word to describe my emotions when I saw the blue screen of death flashing before my eyes. I had spent a hundred hours writing and rewriting the book, and it vanished in the blink of an eye.

I prayed. That didn't work. I asked others to pray, but the blue screen of death flashed in my face like a defiant child. Next, I consulted with technology experts about recovering the book files. I spoke with several companies who offered nothing more than an apology because they could not help.

Finally, I bumped into what looked like a miracle amid the mess. I found a data recovery firm that guaranteed to retrieve all the files on my hard drive—or give me my money back. Although the fee was a steep $2,000, it was my only hope. With a prayer, I sent them the hard drive and waited. And waited. And waited. I waited for what felt like months.

Weeks later, the company sent me a link to the recovered files. I danced for joy until I realized my book was not in the files. In fact, my book was the only file missing! I couldn't have been clearer when I shelled out $2,000: I need to recover the book. The rest doesn't matter. I double- and triple-checked the files, and the book was missing from the lineup.

I was sure it was an oversight, so I politely asked the technician to look for the book file. He stubbornly refused. When I asked the company to honor its money-back guarantee, the owner rejected my plea. When I told him I would dispute the charge with my credit card company, he confidently told me no one had ever been successful in getting their money back. (Sound familiar?)

My emotions shifted from desperate to angry. I prayed over the issue and vowed to the Lord that I would sow the recovered money into a ministry if He vindicated me from what amounted to theft. This was not a hard vow to make. After all, it wasn't my money to begin with. Everything we have belongs to God.

God heard my prayer. I found favor with my credit card company. Within a month, I got every penny back. Just as I had vowed, I sowed that $2,000 into a ministry and saw one of the greatest harvests I had seen at that time. God also directed my steps to another data recovery company that was able to restore the manuscript for a few hundred dollars.

A PRICELESS LESSON

As harrowing as it was, this experience gave me a testimony to share with my then seven-year-old daughter when someone stole her money out of the community laundry room in our condo.

She loved to help me do the laundry (that changed when she was around thirteen), but in her rush to get back to the condo before a commercial break ended on the program she was watching, she left her purse on the dryer. When she realized she had left it behind a few minutes later, she went back to the laundry room. The purse was long gone. She couldn't believe someone who lived on our floor would steal her money. At that moment, I taught her how to pray for vindication from thieves.

I gave her this scripture to hang her faith on: "People do not despise a thief if he steals to satisfy himself when he is starving. Yet when he is found, he must restore sevenfold; he may have to give up all the substance of his house" (Prov. 6:30–31). She believed it. She prayed it—and within two weeks, she found $120 on the playground.

Being an honest child, she immediately took the money to her teacher, who checked with the groundskeeper. At the end of the day, no one claimed it, and she came home with more than a sevenfold return and a testimony she'd never forget. God can vindicate you from thieves, and it starts with positioning yourself for payback.

TAKE RESPONSIBILITY

Part of positioning yourself for payback is taking responsibility for your mistakes. I'm sure God tried to warn me not to use that data recovery firm, for example, but somehow I missed the heads-up. Before I saw vindication, I had to take responsibility. As a steward of His finances, I had to repent. I couldn't blame the thieves for acting like thieves. The thief always comes to steal, kill, and destroy (John 10:10).

Making poor decisions can open a door for the enemy to work his wicked ministry in our lives. Repenting puts us back in a power position. Proverbs 28:13 says, "Whoever conceals his transgressions will not prosper, but he who confesses and forsakes them will obtain mercy" (ESV). When that data firm took my money and didn't deliver the book, I needed God's mercy. I needed His vindication. God's path to restoration begins with repentance.

Adam and Eve took a different stance. The snake in the garden deceived Eve, but Adam ate freely of the forbidden fruit. When God confronted Adam and Eve, they played the blame game. Genesis 3:12–13 recounts the first couple's excuses to God: "'The woman whom you gave to be with me, she gave me fruit of the tree, and I ate.' Then the LORD God said to the woman, 'What is this that you have done?' The woman said, 'The serpent deceived me, and I ate.'"

Despite the enemy's handiwork, God still held Adam and Eve responsible. As long as you blame others for your poor decision making, you will never grow. The devil can't *make* you do anything. Repent to the Lord for your part and align with His vindication promises. Acts 3:19 promises, "Repent, then, and turn to God, so that your sins may be wiped out, that times of refreshing may come from the Lord." Vindication is part of that refreshing.

REJECT GUILT, SHAME, AND CONDEMNATION

Once you repent, you need to let it go and trust God for vindication. Don't keep beating yourself up like I did many years ago. I was serving under a pastor who was pressuring people in the congregation to buy property at the height of the market in 2005. Since I had no credit, I wasn't in a position to get a loan. The church administrator had a bright idea: if I put up the money, she would put up the credit. I naively agreed, and we formed a partnership.

The house we purchased as a rental property to drive passive revenue streams turned out to be a money pit that sucked the financial life out of me. Beyond the $20,000 I put down to get the loan, I had to pay for one repair after another—after another. By the time I pulled out of the deal, I had lost $100,000. I knew I had made a bad decision. I beat myself up for years over that. The enemy told me I was a poor steward and repeatedly reminded me how I could have used that money for my daughter's college. It was hard to let go.

Finally, the Holy Spirit stepped in and reminded me of Romans 8:1: "There is therefore now no condemnation to those who are in Christ Jesus, who do not walk according to the flesh, but according to the Spirit." God is not condemning you for making poor decisions that bring you loss, though He wants you to learn from it and rise higher. I finally got over it, and looking back, I could see how the guilt, shame, and condemnation hindered my vindication.

Did you get that? I said guilt, shame, and condemnation were hindering my vindication. I didn't have faith in God for payback because it was my fault in the first place. I invested with a clean heart, though, and God looks at the heart. I truly thought I was doing the right thing. In time, I learned to stand on Romans 8:28: "And we know that all things work together for good to them that love God, to them who are the called according to his purpose."

God did vindicate me, knowing I was young, naïve, and highly pressured to do that real estate deal. Over the years, spectacular real estate investment deals started coming my way. I always prayed about whether to invest and waited on the Lord. Today, I own four properties—all paid for in cash. Some of the properties are rented and create passive revenue streams for me. I was surely vindicated, but I had to ask for and receive God's forgiveness first.

PRAY FOR JUSTICE

Assuming you've met the vindication conditions in chapter 5, you can ask the Lord for justice—more than once if you have to. Consider again the parable of the persistent widow.

> [Jesus] told them a parable to the effect that they ought always to pray and not to turn coward (faint, lose heart, and give up). He said, In a certain city there was a judge who neither reverenced and

feared God nor respected or considered man. And there was a widow in that city who kept coming to him and saying, Protect and defend and give me justice against my adversary.

And for a time he would not; but later he said to himself, Though I have neither reverence or fear for God nor respect or consideration for man, yet because this widow continues to bother me, I will defend and protect and avenge her, lest she give me intolerable annoyance and wear me out by her continual coming or at the last she come and rail on me or assault me or strangle me.

Then the Lord said, Listen to what the unjust judge says! And will not [our just] God defend and protect and avenge His elect (His chosen ones), who cry to Him day and night? Will He defer them and delay help on their behalf? I tell you, He will defend and protect and avenge them speedily. However, when the Son of Man comes, will He find [persistence in] faith on the earth?

—LUKE 18:1–9, AMPC

Declare that He will find faith in you for payback.

CHAPTER 14

FROM INSULT TO INCREASE

ROBERT FROST WAS holding a public reading of his celebrated poetry when an audience member in the back of the theater had the audacity to get up and walk out. As Frost watched him exit the building, the literary legend was so insulted he threw his collection of poems at the man. Frost's outrage didn't end there. He found out the man's name and took swift revenge. That man was Truman Capote.

Capote, who went on to be one of the most recognized American novelists, screenwriters, and playwrights of the twentieth century, insisted he never meant to insult the poetry master. He had the flu and left in the middle of Frost's performance because he felt too sick to stay.

Frost could not be consoled. He called Harold Ross, *The New Yorker*'s founding editor, and demanded Capote be fired from his job as a copyboy. The young writer then found himself jobless. Capote later told *Esquire* magazine Frost "was the meanest man who ever drew breath, an old fake dragging around with a shaggy head of hair followed by pathetic old ladies from the Middle West."[1] Now that's insulting!

WHEN YOU SUFFER INSULTS

Not a week goes by that someone doesn't make a YouTube video insulting me. Part of the onslaught is because I am a woman in ministry. I've learned that the more influence God gives you, the more insults come against you. I've learned to let mean-spirited words roll off my back.

Don't get me wrong; I don't enjoy reading insulting comments about myself. I've taken on the late faith healer Kathryn Kuhlman's philosophy. I don't read anything that puffs me up or tears me down. Of course, sometimes it's unavoidable. You can't escape every insult. There's always someone who doesn't like you and makes sure you know why.

When you look at the meaning of *insult*, it's pretty intense. It means "to treat with insolence, indignity, or contempt...to affect offensively or damagingly...an instance of insolent or contemptuous speech or conduct... and something that causes or has the potential for causing such injury," according to *Merriam-Webster*'s dictionary.[2] An insult isn't too far off, then, from a curse. A curse is an invocation that aims to bring harm or injury to someone.

Thank God, He tells us what to do when we are insulted—and He tells us how to set ourselves up for increase in the face of insults. Peter was speaking of Jesus when he wrote, "When He was reviled, did not revile in return; when He suffered, He did not threaten, but committed Himself to Him who judges righteously" (1 Pet. 2:23). When someone insults you, commit yourself to the righteous judge. He will vindicate you.

GREAT IS YOUR REWARD

It's hard to imagine how an insult could lead to a blessing. But that's just how God works. First Peter 4:14 tells us, "If you are reproached for the name of Christ, blessed are you, for the Spirit of glory and of God rests upon you." When someone insults you, go ahead and declare that the spirit of glory is resting on you.

Jesus went on to say, "Blessed are you when they revile and persecute you, and say all kinds of evil against you falsely for My sake. Rejoice and be exceedingly glad, for great is your reward in heaven, for so they persecuted the prophets who were before you" (Matt. 5:11–12). Start rejoicing now because the insult is opening the door to increase.

But again, we have to pray for those who insult us. Jesus, the just judge, is grieved when people insult us for following His leadership. When you are living for Him, the insult against you is an insult against Him. Jesus said, "If you call someone an idiot, you are in danger of being brought before the court. And if you curse someone, you are in danger of the fires of hell" (Matt. 5:22, NLT). Pray for those who insult you and curse you. They are standing in a dangerous place.

PRESSING PAST PUBLIC INSULTS

David was insulted over and over again, but one incident in particular drives home the point I want to make: the insult will lead to your increase. God will turn the curse into a blessing if you respond rightly.

Imagine the scene: David was weeping and barefoot as

he left Jerusalem. His son Absalom had just launched a coup. David didn't want to see the city destroyed, so he left willingly, only to meet with a man from the house of Saul who came out to add insult to injury. We read the account in 2 Samuel 16:5–8:

> Now when King David came to Bahurim, there was a man from the family of the house of Saul, whose name was Shimei the son of Gera, coming from there. He came out, cursing continuously as he came. And he threw stones at David and at all the servants of King David. And all the people and all the mighty men were on his right hand and on his left.
>
> Also Shimei said thus when he cursed: "Come out! Come out! You bloodthirsty man, you rogue! The Lord has brought upon you all the blood of the house of Saul, in whose place you have reigned; and the Lord has delivered the kingdom into the hand of Absalom your son. So now you are caught in your own evil, because you are a bloodthirsty man!"

Some translations say Shimei shouted insults.

FOCUS ON THE VINDICATOR

David's clan was so incensed they wanted to take off Shimei's head! But David took the insults in stride. He even suggested the Lord may have sent Shimei to heap curses on his head. The point is that David didn't retaliate. Amid the insults, Absalom's betrayal, and his personal grief, David kept his eyes on the God who had always been faithful to vindicate him.

David said, "Let him alone, and let him curse; for so the LORD has ordered him. It may be that the LORD will look on my affliction, and that the LORD will repay me with good for his cursing this day" (2 Sam. 16:11–12). David's righteous heart attitude didn't immediately change the situation. Shimei went along the hillside opposite David and continued cursing him, throwing stones at him, and kicking up dust. But David kept quiet.

When people are insulting and cursing us, we can't allow ourselves to grow weary in well doing. And we can't return evil for evil. David could have had Shimei silenced, but he trusted the same God who helped him overcome the lion, the bear, Goliath, and Saul's murder attempts against his life. He was waiting for God to turn the curse into a blessing. God is just that good, and David knew it.

WHEN THE CURSE BECOMES A BLESSING

Perhaps David was inspired by Deuteronomy 23:5, when God turned Balaam's curse into a blessing because of His love for the Israelites. The Israelites didn't deserve the curse of Balaam, and the curse causeless does not land. (See Proverbs 26:2.) Balaam knew this, saying, "How shall I curse whom God has not cursed? And how shall I denounce whom the LORD has not denounced?" (Num. 23:8).

When people curse you without a cause, pray for them. Jesus said, "Bless those who curse you" (Luke 6:28). Paul put it this way: "Bless, and curse not" (Rom. 12:14, KJV). When you take on this attitude, like David, the curse cannot land but it may rebound on the sender because they will reap what they sow.

Keep your heart right. Forgive them. Pray for mercy and ask God to forgive them, because although they may be insulting you maliciously, they don't ultimately understand what they are doing. In this way, you return good for evil and set yourself up for promotion.

CHAPTER 15

REACH OUT YOUR HAND

I T WAS ONE of the most important relationships of my life—a friendship that bore much fruit over many years. But a sharp disagreement strained the pact. Strife opened the door for the enemy to break the bond. Unity was traded for animosity, and the fractured friendship led to a spiritual family feud.

People who knew us both felt forced to take sides. Suddenly I had a slew of friends-turned-enemies. I kept my mouth shut and said little to anyone except the two people closest to me, who I knew would be faithful to pray. The continual stream of gossip and slander against me was vitriolic, and it always seemed to get back to me.

Two years later, we both recognized a breach in the spirit the enemy was using to harm us, the people around us, and our ministries. We had a private meeting, put all the knives out on the table, and allowed the Holy Spirit to show us how the enemy infiltrated the friendship. After two hours in a coffee shop in a neutral city—face to face—God exposed the enemy and vindicated the relationship. Humility was the pathway to vindication.

WHEN SEPARATIONS TURN HATEFUL

John, the apostle of love, inked some strong words that should spur us to reevaluate our love walk, especially in the face of separation: "If someone says, 'I love God,' and hates his brother, he is a liar; for he who does not love his brother whom he has seen, how can he love God whom he has not seen?" (1 John 4:20).

In this era of Christianity, I'm seeing offense and division on the rise among believers—even among ministers of the gospel. I don't see this level of fallout between friends in the Bible, even when there was a sharp disagreement. Consider Paul and Barnabas, who had a serious falling out.

> After some time Paul said to Barnabas, "Let's go back and visit each city where we previously preached the word of the Lord, to see how the new believers are doing." Barnabas agreed and wanted to take along John Mark. But Paul disagreed strongly, since John Mark had deserted them in Pamphylia and had not continued with them in their work.
>
> Their disagreement was so sharp that they separated. Barnabas took John Mark with him and sailed for Cyprus. Paul chose Silas, and as he left, the believers entrusted him to the Lord's gracious care. Then he traveled throughout Syria and Cilicia, strengthening the churches there.
>
> —ACTS 15:36–41, NLT

Paul and Barnabas agreed to disagree and went their separate ways. These anointed men of God didn't try to tear each other's ministry down. In fact, Paul later told the church at Corinth Barnabas' ministry was worthy of support (1 Cor. 9:6). Paul later told the church at Colossae to welcome John Mark if he showed up in their midst (Col. 4:10). And Paul even requested John Mark's presence in his second letter to Timothy, though Bible scholars say this was likely a decade later after Mark matured (2 Tim. 4:11).

Likewise, when Abraham and Lot separated, they didn't try to destroy each other's reputation with secret statements and not-so-secret phone calls casting aspersions of wrongdoing on innocent hands. No, Abraham actually went to war to rescue Lot from danger (Gen. 14) and later interceded for his life when God set out to destroy Sodom (Gen. 18:22–19:29). This is true love.

WALKING IN LOVE DURING DISAGREEMENT

Whether it's leaving a church, divorcing a spouse, quitting a job, or cutting ties with a once-best friend, so often Christians choose to launch social media smear campaigns and cast aspersions on a person's character and motives instead of just going their way with a blessing. The Holy Spirit whispered these words to me decades ago: "It's not about being right. It's about being righteous." If we want reconciliation, we need to swallow our pride.

Beloved, strife is an abomination to God (Prov. 6:16–19). Strife affects the anointing and the flow of the Holy Ghost (Ps. 133:1–3). Strife grieves the Holy Spirit (Eph. 4:30). Strife destroys relationships (Prov. 17:9). Strife is rooted in anger (Prov. 29:22), hatred (Prov. 10:12), pride (Prov. 13:10), and a quarrelsome, self-seeking spirit (Gal. 5:14–18; Luke 22:24–27).

We need to learn to walk in love even when we can't walk in agreement. Let's not return evil for evil, but return good for evil, even if it's only through our prayers. Choose humility. This sets the stage for vindication in relationships the enemy damaged. Remember, blessed are the peacemakers, for they will be called the children of God (Matt. 5:9). Be a peacemaker. If you are going to strive, strive to be at peace with all men as far as it depends on you (Rom. 12:18).

THAT FAMOUS CHRISTIAN

Some years ago, I was invited to speak on a strategic conference call with key leaders in the body of Christ. I was honored—and excited—until I learned a woman of God who was holding a mystery grudge against me was also set to speak. The host had no idea there was a conflict between us. I gave him the background because he was a longtime friend, and I didn't want to put him in an awkward position.

"I don't know what Sarah has against me," I said, "but I've been told there is a significant issue. I'll bow out of the call to avoid an undercurrent of strife in the meeting." How did I know Sarah had an issue with me? It wasn't my imagination. It was obvious the first time I met her in a small green room at a television studio.

Well, technically, I never "met" Sarah. When she saw me in the green room, her face suddenly transformed from a bright smile to a harsh glare. Sarah sat in a chair and intentionally turned her body away from me. For thirty minutes, she would not acknowledge my presence.

It was as if I wasn't in the room. I was beyond uncomfortable but stayed quiet.

I left the studio wondering what in the world was going on. I had no idea what was wrong until a year later when a Christian producer offered me a free year of programming on his network. Just before the deal was signed, I got a call. The producer told me Sarah blocked the deal. Sarah told the decision makers that I had wronged her, and they pulled my contract out of respect for her. When the producer asked Sarah what I had done, she said, "Jennifer knows what she did." I honestly had no idea what she was talking about—and I was angry.

Now back to the conference call. When I found out Sarah was going to be on the broadcast, I bowed out. When the host asked why, I told him how Sarah had something against me, but I had no idea what it could be. Within minutes, the conference host contacted Sarah and asked her what the problem was—then relayed it to me. I was shocked. I did nothing even close to what she described.

I was told Sarah would drop the issue if I apologized. That made me even angrier because not only was I innocent, but I realized she had been mercilessly slamming doors of opportunity in my face for years. I wanted to say plenty of things to Sarah, but "I'm sorry" wasn't one of them.

James teaches us, "Human anger does not produce the righteousness God desires" (1:20, NLT). I was angry, so I kept my mouth shut. I processed it with God for a couple of weeks. I didn't feel I should apologize to this woman. I felt she should apologize to me. Finally, one day, I heard

God's still, small voice say, "I'm trying to promote you." With that, I humbled myself and called Sarah. I let her share everything she thought I did for about twenty minutes. When I explained my side, she believed, forgave, and befriended me. And God vindicated and promoted me speedily.

REACH OUT YOUR HAND

Relational vindication often demands someone take the first step toward reconciliation. The enemy withers relationships through misunderstandings, betrayals, and other wiles, but acting in humility can break the enemy's back and release vindication. After all, God gives grace to the humble (1 Pet. 5:5).

Of course, some people just won't reconcile with you, no matter how kind, loving, or humble you are toward them. That's why Hebrews 12:14 says, "Make every effort to live in peace with everyone and to be holy; without holiness no one will see the Lord" (NIV). Sometimes, despite your best efforts, the other party will slap your hand away.

However, I've learned if you make a sincere effort, sometimes God will move on even the hardest hearts. God showed me a clear strategy to heal withered relationships and release vindication among friendships: reach out your hand. Consider this passage in Mark 3:1–5 (TLB):

> While in Capernaum Jesus went over to the synagogue again, and noticed a man there with a deformed hand. Since it was the Sabbath, Jesus'

enemies watched him closely. Would he heal the man's hand? If he did, they planned to arrest him!

Jesus asked the man to come and stand in front of the congregation. Then turning to his enemies he asked, "Is it all right to do kind deeds on Sabbath days? Or is this a day for doing harm? Is it a day to save lives or to destroy them?"

But they wouldn't answer him. Looking around at them angrily, for he was deeply disturbed by their indifference to human need, he said to the man, "Reach out your hand." He did, and instantly his hand was healed!

Sometimes when you reach out your hand, the relationship is immediately healed. Even though it looked impossible, even though you thought the enemy had destroyed all hope of restoration, reaching out your hand can defeat the handiwork of the wicked one to steal, kill, and destroy relationships.

CHAPTER 16

FACING THE ACCUSER

Ronnie Wallace Long spent forty-four years behind bars based on an intentional false accusation. At age twenty-one, the Black Concord, North Carolina, resident was accused of raping a White woman—and an all-White jury decided beyond a shadow of a doubt he was guilty. Long was convicted of burglary and rape in 1976 and received two life sentences.

It was a setup, according to the attorneys who picked up his wrongful incarceration lawsuit decades later. Long's attorneys argued local law enforcement leaders handpicked the jury. The investigation revealed more than forty fingerprints collected from the crime scene did not match Long's. Other evidence that could have helped Long either was not disclosed or simply disappeared.

After spending forty-four years in prison, Long was exonerated in 2020. But he wasn't just exonerated, he was vindicated. The sixty-eight-year-old received a $25 million settlement. "I know my mother and father died with a broken heart," Long told CBS News. "I'm gonna tell them now, when I visit the gravesite, 'Your son is clear.'"[1]

While $25 million doesn't make up for nearly a lifetime behind bars, it is vindication—and it helps us put the false accusations against us into perspective. We are not likely to go to jail for decades based on a false accusation (although I did spend forty days there).

False accusations are essentially character assassinations. *Merriam-Webster*'s dictionary defines *assassination* as "murder by sudden or secret attack often for political reasons."[2] While murder can be accidental—that's called manslaughter—assassination is always premeditated. Character assassins know exactly what they are doing. Their words are calculated to sully your good name.

A study from Vanderbilt University reveals that making accusations of unethical business practices makes the accuser look more trustworthy while the accused appears untrustworthy. What's more, people who hear the accusation are more likely to reward the accusers.[3] The bottom line: accusations—whether true or false—lift up the accuser and tear down the accused in the ears of those who listen.

The word *assassination* also means "treacherous destruction of a person's reputation."[4] Indeed, most people aren't slinging guns; they are using spiritual slingshots and stones of accusation to damage their target's good name. Whether inside or outside of the church, assassins do their dirty work through accusations, gossip, and setups. Assassins frame people for sins they did not commit, cast aspersions on people who did no wrong, and otherwise fabricate stories to gain a critical mass of people to their side.

I've experienced character assassination many times over the years. I've been accused of being underhanded and lacking common decency. I've been accused of having a Jezebel spirit, splitting churches, breaking into churches, cussing out pastors, and more. But God always vindicates me from false accusations. Of course, sometimes the process takes longer than at other times.

THE DANGER OF FALSE ACCUSATIONS

False accusations are dangerous. Exodus 23:1 warns us not to spread a false report and not to cooperate with evil people by lying. Proverbs 6:19 tells us a false witness who breathes lies is an abomination to the Lord. And Proverbs 19:9 clearly warns us a false witness will be punished and a liar destroyed. That's intense!

With these verses in mind, make sure your heart is clean before you set out to pray for vindication over false accusations against you. It's been said a clear conscience laughs at a false accusation. On the other hand, you won't see vindication in your life if you have vindictively accused others and expressed no repentance. In fact, your false accusations of others may have opened the door to false accusations against you. Selah. When you act like the accuser of the brethren, he has a legal right to attack you on many fronts.

Sit with the Lord and spend some time thinking and praying. Ask the Lord to show you if you have agreed with the accuser. If you have, quickly repent. Ask God to forgive you for any times you've made false accusations against others, knowingly or unknowingly, through repeating or agreeing with gossip. Once you break your agreement with the accuser, you are in line for vindication from false accusations.

MOSES MODELS THE WAY

False accusations are often rooted in jealousy. Moses could tell you stories. I'll tell you one for him. Moses handpicked Korah for the special privilege of ministering in the Tabernacle, but that wasn't enough to put out the fire of jealousy in his heart. Korah organized two hundred fifty congregational leaders in a coup against Moses and Aaron—and false accusations were at the center of the campaign.

Listen in: "They gathered together against Moses and Aaron, and said to them, 'You take too much upon yourselves, for all the congregation is holy, every one of them, and the LORD is among them. Why then do you exalt yourselves above the assembly of the LORD?'" (Num. 16:3). And again, "Is it a small thing that you have brought us up out of a land flowing with milk and honey, to kill us in the wilderness, that you should keep acting like a prince over us? Moreover you have not brought us into a land flowing with milk and honey, nor given us inheritance of fields and vineyards" (Num. 16:13–14).

Moses got mad! He ran to the Lord and flat out told Him they were lying. God responded with the promise of swift vindication. He told Moses and Aaron to "separate yourselves from among this congregation, that I may consume them in a moment" (Num. 16:21). This, of course, was a test. God wanted to see what was in Moses' heart. Moses fell on his face and prayed for the innocent ones among the congregation and God spared them— but God's vengeance ultimately fell on Korah. This is the story:

> Now it came to pass, as [Moses] finished speaking
> all these words, that the ground split apart under
> them, and the earth opened its mouth and swal-
> lowed them up, with their households and all the
> men with Korah, with all their goods. So they and
> all those with them went down alive into the pit;
> the earth closed over them, and they perished from
> among the assembly. Then all Israel who were
> around them fled at their cry, for they said, "Lest
> the earth swallow us up also!"
>
> —NUMBERS 16:31

Even after witnessing this dramatic vindication and
Moses' selfless intercession for them, the Israelites went
back to complaining and accusing the leadership. That
kindled the wrath of God, who sent a plague that killed
nearly fifteen thousand people. God takes false accusations seriously.

YOU ARE NOT ALONE

If you've been falsely accused, you are not alone. Satan
accused God of lying to Eve about the tree of the knowledge of good and evil (Gen. 3:1–6). Saul falsely accused
Ahimelech of helping David escape his sword—and killed
him and his family (1 Sam. 22:11–16). Joab falsely accused
Abner of lying about his allegiance to David—and murdered him (1 Sam. 3:24–27). Ahab falsely accused Elijah
of troubling Israel (1 Kings 18:17–18).

But it doesn't stop there. Jezebel launched false
accusations against Naboth that got him murdered
(1 Kings 21:7–13). Sanballat falsely accused Nehemiah
as he worked to rebuild the walls around Jerusalem

(Neh. 6). Jeremiah faced false accusation after false accusation from priests, prophets, and people during his ministry (Jer. 26; 37; 43).

People falsely accused Jesus of being gluttonous and a drunkard (Matt. 11:19). The scribes and Pharisees falsely accused Jesus of blasphemy and said He had a demon (Matt. 12:22–32). False accusations against Him got Him crucified. False witnesses were used against Stephen and incited the people to murder (Acts 6:7–15). The apostle Paul endured tremendous levels of false accusation (Acts 17:7; 21:28; 24:5–6, 13; 25:2, 7; Rom. 3:8). Shall I go on?

EMBRACE THE SPIRIT OF GLORY

Facing false accusations is never fun. As I mentioned, I've faced many. I still remember a man—we'll call him Frank—who was offended because I didn't have time to meet with him during a conference. I already had plans with the guest speakers and had never agreed to meet with Frank, who was a stranger to me. I had, however, agreed to allow him and roughly a dozen of his youths to come to the conference free of charge even though it was sold out.

Most people would have appreciated the gesture, but Frank was so offended that I would not go out to eat with him that he started making all sorts of nasty, false accusations about me and spreading them throughout my region. Frank even called *Charisma* magazine, where I was editor, and some people with whom I was affiliated to bear false witness against me. Little did I know he had partnered with a pastor in the city who was jealous of me to launch his smear campaign.

Frank accused me of many things, but probably the

most ridiculous accusation painted a detailed picture of me getting into a knock-down, drag-out fight with a visitor at my church. However, his fabricated story quickly imploded. I was out of town on the date and time he insisted this occurred.

Several leaders in the body of Christ came to my defense, even rebuking Frank for his false accusations, but he persisted. I kept blessing him and asking God to deal with it. Three years later, Frank wrote a lengthy letter to the ministry apologizing for his behavior and asking how he could make it up to me. Of course, he couldn't make it up to me. Frank destroyed my reputation with a lot of undiscerning people. But the good news is God did make it up to me.

Remember the words of Peter, "If you are reproached for the name of Christ, blessed are you, for the Spirit of glory and of God rests upon you" (1 Pet. 4:14). Pray mercy for those who falsely accuse you because if they don't repent, judgment will fall upon them, but if you keep your heart right, His glory will rest up on you.

CHAPTER 17

WHEN GOD REBUKES THE DEVOURER

H E TOLD ME he wanted us to renew our wedding vows when he returned from Latin America and presented me with diamond earrings. His words were like music to my ears because our marriage was clearly under attack, and he had been unwilling to work on the problems. He was an out-of-work photographer, and I was a thriving journalist. I hoped the trip he took to Latin America to build his photography portfolio would refresh him. But I never saw him again. That was 1999.

When my troubled husband left me and our two-year-old daughter behind to start a new life, he also left behind mountains of debt. He maxed out the credit cards, living the high life with his foreign mistress. And I later discovered he had secretly siphoned many thousands of dollars out of our joint bank account.

To say I was in a financial mess is an understatement. My credit was destroyed. I couldn't get through a single day without nagging calls from a long list of creditors demanding payback for his big spending. Making matters worse, the IRS was coming after me for his tax liabilities. I thought I was going to have to declare bankruptcy.

I thought that was rock bottom, but things went from bad to worse. You know the story: I was falsely accused of a crime I didn't commit and faced ten years in prison. Despite God's vindication, I was nearly penniless when I was released from jail. I had only a few dollars to my name, no place to live, and no prospects for work because the dot-com bubble burst. I moved to a small country town to get a fresh—and affordable—start. I lived an especially meager lifestyle, far below the poverty line amid a recession.

I was beyond stressed out. I was suddenly a single mother. My ex-husband paid no alimony or child support. I ended up on food stamps. I could barely rent a place to live due to the poor credit. I was so poor I let my foot off the gas when driving down a hill to save a few pennies. It was just a mess all the way around—a mess I didn't create and didn't know how to fix. Even still, I was generous with what little I had. I let people borrow money I couldn't afford to lose—but I wasn't giving to God. As a brand-new believer, I didn't know I was supposed to give to God.

A STUNNING, STILL SMALL VOICE

After weeks of waiting for someone to repay me money I loaned them—money I desperately needed to pay my bills—I got on my knees and started crying out to God. I was so angry. I said, "Lord, You see how people are robbing me! I'm tired of people robbing me! It's not fair! It's not right! I am trying to be helpful and generous, and You see where that gets me!" Suddenly I heard the Holy Spirit say, "You are robbing me."

I was stunned. I didn't have any idea what He meant. Seriously. I was clueless. I was giving small offerings at church but didn't know anything about tithes. That's when the Lord took me to Malachi 3:8–12:

> "Will a man rob God? Yet you have robbed Me! But you say, 'In what way have we robbed You?' In tithes and offerings. You are cursed with a curse, for you have robbed Me, even this whole nation. Bring all the tithes into the storehouse, that there may be food in My house, and try Me now in this," says the LORD of hosts, "If I will not open for you the windows of heaven and pour out for you such blessing that there will not be room enough to receive it.
>
> "And I will rebuke the devourer for your sakes, so that he will not destroy the fruit of your ground, nor shall the vine fail to bear fruit for you in the field," says the LORD of hosts; "and all nations will call you blessed, for you will be a delightful land," says the LORD of hosts.

Those verses caused my jaw to drop. I never heard the pastor preach about tithing, but the Holy Spirit became my teacher. I didn't know it at the time, but God was trying to set me up for financial vindication. He was trying to deliver me from the small country town to the high-rise on a South Florida beach, cancel all my debt, and give me real estate investments, savings accounts, and more.

God had already given me the power to create wealth to establish His covenant in the earth.

(See Deuteronomy 8:18.) Now He was showing me how to activate that power—and it all started with giving Him the tithe.

DOUBLE RESTORATION IS YOURS

Financial vindication—even double restoration—can be yours. This is a biblical principle, and we see it in the story of a wealthy Shunammite woman who honored a prophet. This generous woman set up "prophet's quarters" on her roof so Elisha would have a place to rest when he was passing through her region.

Hoping to return the kindness, Elisha later prophesied the wealthy woman would give birth to a son. A son would be a blessing since she was childless and her husband was much older. The Shunammite gave birth to a baby boy the next year. Some years later, the boy tragically died working in the field with his father. The bereaved mother was understandably devastated, but Elisha was not the least bit rattled. He immediately traveled to her home and raised the boy from the dead. (See 2 Kings 4.)

That would have served as a happy ending, but that wasn't the end of the story. Sometime later, Elisha saw a famine coming to the land. Not only did he warn the woman, but he also offered her a survival strategy straight from heaven. Second Kings 8:1–2 lays it out: "Arise and go, you and your household, and stay wherever you can; for the LORD has called for a famine, and furthermore, it will come upon the land for seven years.' So the woman arose and did according to the saying of the man of God, and she went with her household and dwelt in the land of the Philistines seven years."

The Shunammite woman believed the prophet and prospered, but her property was seized while she hunkered down in Philistia for seven years. Perhaps strangers—squatters—had taken possession of her land. Or maybe a neighboring landowner expanded onto her property, thinking she would not return. But she did return—and marched right into the presence of the king to demand her land back. As divine providence would have it, God ordered her steps to the king with miraculous timing. Second Kings 8:4–6 tells the whole story.

> Then the king talked with Gehazi, the servant of the man of God, saying, "Tell me, please, all the great things Elisha has done." Now it happened, as he was telling the king how he had restored the dead to life, that there was the woman whose son he had restored to life, appealing to the king for her house and for her land.
>
> And Gehazi said, "My lord, O king, this is the woman, and this is her son whom Elisha restored to life." And when the king asked the woman, she told him. So the king appointed a certain officer for her, saying, "Restore all that was hers, and all the proceeds of the field from the day that she left the land until now."

The Shunammite woman not only took her land back—that would have been financial vindication plain and clear—but she also got more than she expected. She got payback with interest. She experienced financial vindication. She never had to work another day in her life.

TAPPING INTO FINANCIAL VINDICATION

Maybe someone harmed your financial status. Maybe you lost everything in a divorce. Maybe a dishonest business partner took off with what belonged to you. Like the Shunammite woman—and like me—you too can see financial vindication in your life. But how?

First, own up to your decisions. Say it out loud, "I am responsible." Those are the first three words you need to say when adversity hits your life. No, I'm not saying you are responsible for all adversity that comes your way. But you are responsible for how you respond to it.

On the other hand, we do sometimes make poor decisions and open the door for the enemy to meddle in our minds. When adversity strikes, the first thing I do is examine my heart. "Am I out of God's will? Did I open a door to the enemy somehow?" Before we start chasing devils, we need to chase God for a revelation of where the trouble lies.

I mentioned this a few chapters back, but it bears repeating: many are tempted to blame shift when things go wrong—pointing fingers at others for their own mistakes, failures, and warfare. This is not a helpful perspective if you want to see things shift because blame is the barrier to change. When you refuse to take responsibility for your part, you hinder your spiritual growth and your natural breakthrough.

Stop beating yourself up, and don't fall for the temptation to blame God. This is a subtle trick the enemy plays on our minds. Think of Job. His wife's best advice when he lost his family and his wealth was to curse God and die. Like Naomi, who lost her husband and her sons and became bitter, Job's wife blamed God for their misfortunes.

God is not the robber. God is the vindicator. John 10:10 makes this absolutely clear: "The thief does not come, except to steal and kill and destroy. I came that they may have life, and that they may have it more abundantly" (MEV).

Job refused to blame God for his misfortunes. He didn't put God on the hook, and everything he lost at the enemy's hand was restored twofold. Once your heart is clean, ask God for financial vindication. That's what I did. Although my husband left me with mountains of debt, God delivered me from it all. Today I am debt-free.

CHAPTER 18

WHEN THE BATTLE RAGES

WHEN GOD CALLED me to make prayer my life's work, I never imagined the level of warfare that would come against my life. I prayed about what God whispered to my heart—"Make prayer your life's work"—for forty days before even trying to take a first step. First, I wasn't sure what it meant to make prayer my life's work. At the time, I was doing many works. Should I quit the editorship at *Charisma* magazine to pray eight hours a day? Should I write books on prayer? What did God really mean?

I prayed about this Holy Spirit commissioning for weeks without telling a soul. After a period of set-aside seeking, I felt the call to build a house of prayer. I had no idea how to do that. Again, I had no idea how much spiritual warfare I'd face when I stepped out in obedience to His leading to launch a prayer ministry.

Call me naïve. I guess I thought God would roll out the red carpet for me, give me the nicest facility in the area, and bring the people in droves to make intercession. It didn't happen that way, but God did bless the work. He opened the door to a small church for our first prayer meeting. I was excited to partner with the pastor to bring more prayer to the region.

We were starting to get some traction in the prayer room when the pastor of the host church began affirming sexual immorality on the platform. My small team was shocked. My worship leader and I had a "come to Jesus" talk with this young pastor, whose mind was clearly under enemy attack. Without a thimbleful of humility, he harshly rebuked us. We knew that spirit would destroy what God was building, so we blessed the man and left the venue.

We later learned this pastor was telling anyone who would listen that I brought division in his church, but not a single soul left his flock to join our house of prayer when we exited. Despite his claims, we continued to bless him.

GOD OPENS DOORS NO MAN CAN SHUT

The enemy thought he could use this pastor to shut down our God-ordained work. The devil thought he could discredit me and cause leaders to shut their hearts—and doors—to the house of prayer. But we knew our God was greater than the accusations being made against me. God vindicated us after much spiritual warfare prayer, binding up false accusations, pushing back darkness trying to encroach upon churches in the region, and breaking hindrances to acquire a new facility. God opened another door to a better building.

The new facility was, at first, a blessing. But pretty soon, the religious spirit that ruled over the denominational campus started to turn on us. They didn't like that we prayed in tongues. They didn't like that I was a woman leading the charge. They didn't like that we worshipped loudly. Suddenly we were forced out of our second home. It seemed like "man" was shutting the door, but it was really God. He sent us there to bless the church, but they rejected the blessing. He delivered us from the persecution and had increase in mind.

We didn't know what we were going to do, so we started praying and warring against the spirit of religion that was working to shut down the only house of prayer in our city. We came against sabotaging demons that were working to stop us from establishing the prayer room. Within weeks of spiritual warfare efforts, God vindicated us. God opened yet another door.

God moved us into a better facility where we established 24/7 prayer. It was a dream come true. Literally. I couldn't believe it. The host refitted a small space on their campus and had plans to build out a larger space complete with state-of-the-art equipment. They even let me tour the megawarehouse they had in mind and detailed the transformation plans. But within a year, God led them to go a different direction.

It was a sudden and major disappointment. But God had a plan. We again went to war. We launched out in spiritual battle and came against twisting spirits that set us up for upset. We decreed and declared the enemy had to flee seven ways. (See Deuteronomy 28:7.) We waged war with the prophetic words spoken over the ministry (1 Tim. 1:18). Within weeks, God opened a door. We ended up in a small storefront retail facility. That's where we started to catch some growth.

THE DEVIL IS IN VIOLATION

Our next facility was like a cracker box—tiny! But we saw miracles, signs, and wonders there. Unfortunately, one of the ministers who had stood with me for several years launched a coup against me. While I was traveling, he took most of our equipment and tried to woo some of our intercessors to his new venture. He did finally return our gear, but his wife called the building code department and waged war against us with false accusations that we were in violation.

Although we were not in violation, when the city official came to do an inspection, he decided the whole building should be brought up to code. That required a wall to be knocked down and wider doors put in. Our landlord was forced to make the upgrades, which left us homeless—and disappointed—once again. But God opened another door. We found a space outfitted as a church in a nearby city. God gave me great favor with the older Jewish woman who owned it. She gave me the building for next to nothing, which was all we could afford—and it was much larger.

FLESH AND BLOOD RISES UP

This was another dream come true, as we were in a desperate situation. The elderly Jewish woman who owned the property liked the idea of having a house of prayer in her building. But warfare arose again. The day before we were supposed to sign the contract, her ultra-Orthodox Jewish son forbade her to put ink to paper because I am a woman leader. He flatly said, "If she truly believes in God, she will understand this and walk away."

I could not believe it. I knew in my heart that we don't wrestle against flesh and blood, but against principalities, powers, rulers of the darkness, and spiritual wickedness in high places (Eph. 6:12). But this lovely woman's son had his own religious beliefs about women in ministry, and we refused to disrespect him.

Once again, our small team launched into spiritual warfare. Every night for seven nights, they marched around the property, claiming it as the house of prayer. Within a week, the elderly woman called weeping, apologizing for her son, and let us rent the building. Finally, after six years, the ministry started growing. We were seeing the prayer room expand by leaps and bounds.

And then the building suddenly collapsed.

I could not believe it. We were on the verge of homelessness when, in the midnight hour, God opened another door. And this one stayed open. We have five times the space we ever had. It's a lovely place in a good location. The enemy finally stopped trying to displace us. But it was a seven-year war.

NO WEAPON FORMED WILL PROSPER

The enemy formed—and deployed—weapon after weapon against us. Oftentimes, those weapons appeared to be prospering. But with every displacement, God taught us how to win wars we'd never fought before. With every displacement, there was a replacement facility that was better than the last one. God kept vindicating us in the warfare and promoting us.

Remember what Isaiah prophesied, "'No weapon formed against you shall prosper, and every tongue which rises against you in judgment You shall condemn. This is the heritage of the servants of the LORD, and their righteousness is from Me,' says the LORD" (Isa. 54:17).

Here's the point: you may not be trying to secure a facility, but perhaps you are trying to secure some other promise. The enemy always resists you, whether it's healing, deliverance, or promotion. But if you stay submitted to God and resist the devil—which is the foundation of all spiritual warfare—He will vindicate you. He will restore what the enemy stole. He will raise you up with more power. He's done it for me time and time again. Fight the good fight of faith while you wait on the Lord. If you don't quit, you'll win.

CHAPTER 19

THE CHILDREN'S BREAD

ONE MINUTE I was fine; the next minute I could barely move. I had black circles under my eyes. My skin was white and pasty. And my body had all but collapsed. I went from preaching on revival circuits every week to being confined to bed most of the day. After weeks of this reality, I was sick, and I was scared.

Doctors could find nothing wrong with me. My bloodwork looked good, but my symptoms persisted. Some days were better than others. At times I thought I was recovering, only to have a setback. At one point I even developed a stutter and a spontaneous twitch in my lip.

A year after the onset of this debilitating attack—after praying, warring, taking communion, and renewing my mind with the Word—I started believing this was my lot in life. Discouraged is not a strong enough word to describe how I felt. Depression was trying to seep in. Despite all this, I kept persevering. I did as much as I could when I could.

Then, in January 2018, the Holy Spirit told me, "When you go to London, you will be healed." Those words were comforting on one hand but frustrating on the other. My trip to London was six months away. It may as well have been six years. I felt like I was losing opportunities and momentum. Many days I was miserable. But I was holding on to the promise of deliverance.

June rolled around, and we set out to Europe. Our first stop was Sweden. I was so exhausted I didn't know how I was going to make it through the rest of the journey. Day by day, I seemed to feel worse and worse. From Sweden, we flew into London, where I rested a couple of days before my next speaking engagement.

On the last day of the journey, the morning of my speaking engagement, I woke up with a headache that was like no other I had ever experienced. It wasn't a mere migraine; it was a spiritual attack of principality proportions. No amount of prayer, medicine, water, or coffee took the edge off. I was in so much pain at one point I wanted to pull my hair out.

Suddenly the pain left as quickly as it came. Within minutes I got a phone call from the conference host saying there was a minister in town who had heard about this debilitating headache and wanted to pray for me. I knew in my spirit this was the moment of deliverance from the mystery ailment. See, I knew all along I wasn't physically sick. Throughout the eighteen months I suffered, I knew this was a satanic attack. I sort of felt like Job in those days. I couldn't make it stop.

After I hung up the phone, I bounded down the stairs to meet with this minister. She started praying for me immediately. She saw little ugly demons all around me in the spirit. She began to break curses—many, many curses. God delivered me from curses from high-level witches and warlocks, and I was immediately healed. So drastic was the change in my appearance that when I got home, people told me I looked ten years younger. And I did!

Maybe there's a curse levied against your life. Or maybe you need deliverance from demon powers that have made their home in your soul from the time you were in your mother's womb. God wants to deliver you from every curse and every tie that binds you. Indeed, your deliverance is vindication from the demons that have tormented you.

MARY MAGDALENE'S BONDAGE

We know Mary Magdalene's story, but we don't know her history. Some claim Mary was a prostitute before she met Jesus, but most serious theologians dismiss that interpretation. Here's what we do know: Mary couldn't have reached the fullness of her destiny in the condition she was in when Jesus found her. Luke 8:1–2 tells the story of Mary's first encounter with Jesus:

> Now it came to pass, afterward, that He went through every city and village, preaching and bringing the glad tidings of the kingdom of God. And the twelve were with Him, and certain women who had been healed of evil spirits and infirmities— Mary called Magdalene, out of whom had come seven demons.

Charles Spurgeon, a nineteenth-century English Baptist preacher, wrote these profound words about Mary Magdalene's experience. You may relate to these words: "She was overwhelmed with seven seas of agony, loaded with seven manacles of despair, encircled with seven walls of fire. Neither day nor night afforded her rest, her brain was on fire, and her soul foamed like a boiling caldron. Miserable soul! No dove of hope brought the olive branch of peace to her forlorn spirit, she sat in the darkness and saw no light—her dwelling was in the valley of the shadow of death."[1]

Spurgeon went on to say:

> Among all the women of Magdala there was none more wretched than she, the unhappy victim of restless and malicious demons. Those who were possessed with these evil spirits, were defiled thereby, as well as made unhappy; for a heart cannot become a kennel for the hounds of hell without being rendered filthy and polluted. I suppose that in addition to the natural corruptions which would be in Mary as well us in ourselves, there would be a more than human nimbleness to evil, a vivacity, an outspokenness bout all her sinful propensities, which only the indwelling fiend could give.
>
> Satan being within, would be sure to stir up the coals of impure thoughts and evil desires, so that the fire of sin would burn vehemently. Her inner self may have been sorely troubled with such excess of wickedness, but she was without power to damp the furnace of her mind. She would be incessantly assaulted by unearthly profanities and hideous suggestions; not as with us, proceeding from the devil without, who is a dreaded antagonist, but from seven devils within, who had entrenched themselves upon a dreadful vantage ground. She was in that sense, no doubt, greatly polluted, although it

would be difficult to say how far she was account-
able for it, on account of the dislodgment of her
reason....

Magdalene's case was a perfectly helpless one;
men could do nothing for her. All the surgery
and physic in the world would have been wasted
upon her singular malady. Had it been any form
of physical disease or purely mental derangement,
help might have been attainable, but who is a
match for the crafty and cruel fiends of the pit?
No drugs can lull them to sleep, no knife can tear
them from the soul.

The loving friend and the skillful adviser stood
equally powerless, nonplussed, bewildered, dismayed. Mary was in a hopeless condition. There
was nothing known by any, even the wise men of
the east, of any method by which seven evil spirits
could be dislodged. However expensive the remedy,
liner relatives would have resorted to it; but who
can cope with devils?

Doubtless all who knew her thought that death
would be a great relief to her, and would relieve
her family of wearisome anxiety and fear. Although
willing to help, they could not aid in the slightest
degree, and had the hourly sorrow of seeing her
endure an agony which they could not alleviate.

Magdalene was the victim of Satanic influence
in a most fearful form: sevenfold were the spirits
which possessed her; and there are men and women
nowadays who are tempted by the great enemy of
souls to a most awful degree. Some of us have
endured temporary seasons of frightful depression,
which have qualified us to sympathize with those

who are more constantly lashed by the fury of the infernal powers. We too have had our horror of great darkness.[2]

SUDDEN VINDICATION

We don't know what demons held Mary captive. Some believe it was spirits of infirmity. Some insist the seven devils were seven princes of hell. In reality, it doesn't matter what those demons were. If it were important that we know, God would have told us. The point is she encountered Jesus, who went about doing good and healing all who were oppressed by the devil (Acts 10:38).

Mary was demonized, and suddenly she was vindicated from the demons that held her in bondage. Suddenly she was walking closely with Jesus. Suddenly she found herself at the foot of the cross where Jesus was being crucified. Suddenly she was positioned to be the first one to share the good news that Jesus had risen from the grave. Suddenly she became an icon in the New Testament church.

What vindication! Whatever demonic attack or curse with which the enemy has afflicted you, Jesus is the deliverer. He came to set the captives free. He came to liberate you from bondage. He came to vindicate you from the enemy. Maybe it will be for you as it was for me. Maybe, as with me, it will be a suddenly!

CHAPTER 20

WHEN VINDICATION IS HEALING

STILL CRY WHEN I watch the video from the Bay of the Holy Spirit Revival in which a paraplegic named Delia Knox got up out of a wheelchair and started walking. Delia was paralyzed in a 1987 accident when a drunk driver struck a car she was in with her sister and brother-in-law. When she woke up in the hospital, she was paralyzed from the waist down. Doctors said she would likely be confined to a wheelchair for the rest of her life.

A successful gospel singer before the accident, Delia continued praising God from her wheelchair and held tight to her faith that she would walk again. Over the years, many people released healing prayers over Delia with no visible results. Then it happened. One fateful day, twenty-three years after the accident, Delia and her husband attended a revival in Alabama. Nathan Morris was preaching. The evangelist prayed over Delia with a determination to see her made whole. As he did, her faith arose.

Soon, Delia could feel her hands resting on her legs. Next, she tried to take a few steps before stumbling and falling back into the wheelchair. As she describes it, doubt started plaguing her mind. But she refused to walk away from her *kairos* time—"when conditions are right for the accomplishment of a crucial action."[1] She got back up again and took a few steps. She started moving her knees up and down, in awe as she went. She walked back and forth with support from bystanders. Over the next few weeks, God strengthened her legs, and she soon started walking alone. She's been walking ever since.

"The miracle is the journey. It's not the moment. It's the journey of recognizing who God is. If He would have never healed me, I would still be pushing through to get into His face," Knox said. "Because it's not about the healing; it's about the journey of knowing that God is there for us."[2]

REJECTING EVIL REPORTS

I call this healing vindication. When tragedies happen or when the doctor gives us a bad report, fear often starts screaming at our souls. The enemy thinks he has the upper hand. But God has promised no weapon formed against us—including sickness and disease—shall prosper (Isa. 54:17). Infirmity is a weapon of the enemy that may seem to prosper for a season—even a long season. But God's healing power can vindicate us.

Let me state this emphatically: it's not God's will for us to live sick, diseased, or paralyzed. He is the Lord that heals us (Exod. 15:26). He is the Lord who forgives our sins and heals all our diseases (Ps. 103:1–3). Jesus bore our sickness on the cross (Isa. 53:4–5). Remember, "God anointed Jesus of Nazareth with the Holy Spirit and with power, who went about doing good and healing all who were oppressed by the devil, for God was with Him" (Acts 10:28).

If you've had a setback in your health—even if you treated your body roughly, didn't eat or sleep right, and so on—God can still heal you. He's just that good. Your part is to repent for not taking care of your temple, start renewing your mind to God's healing power, and extend your faith to believe. God can and wants to restore your health. In Jeremiah 30:17, God said, "For I will restore health to you and heal you of your wounds."

TAKING BODY HITS

Many times, infirmity strikes seemingly out of nowhere. When I was seven years old and then again at eight years old, I broke my leg in a freak accident. Both times, I was in traction in the hospital for months with excruciating pain that left my pillow soaked in tears. Both times, I was in a body cast for months. Both times, I had to learn how to walk all over again. I was isolated and felt alone in the hospital, with only the television to keep me company. I was in bed for weeks at home, watching the neighborhood kids play outside through my window. It was a lonely period in my young life.

When the enemy attacks our physical bodies, we must stand for vindication. Job suffered many things. Satan attacked his character. He lost his property and his children. And when he refused to curse God and die, Satan attacked his health. Satan asked permission from God to attack his bones and his flesh, assuming that would be enough to destroy Job.

Listen in to Job 2:6–8: "And the LORD said to Satan,

'Behold, he is in your hand, but spare his life.' So Satan went out from the presence of the LORD, and struck Job with painful boils from the sole of his foot to the crown of his head. And he took for himself a potsherd with which to scrape himself while he sat in the midst of the ashes."

Like Delia Knox, Job suffered. He suffered an extreme case of leprosy in which his skin became elephant-like with cracks and sores. Job said, "My flesh is caked with worms and dust, my skin is cracked and breaks out afresh" (Job 7:5). He also said, "And now my soul is poured out because of my plight; the days of affliction take hold of me. My bones are pierced in me at night, and my gnawing pains take no rest. By great force my garment is disfigured" (Job 30:16–19).

Can you hear the agony in his heart? Nevertheless, Job held on to faith in God as his vindicator—and his health was restored. Job lived to be one hundred forty years old and saw his children and grandchildren for four generations. Job 42:17 tells us he died old and full of days. He was fully vindicated from Satan's attacks throughout the generations of those who read his story.

TOUCHING THE VINDICATOR'S HEART

Job's steadfast faith touched God's heart. Of course, God knew all along the servant about whom he bragged to Satan would make it through the fiery trial. In fact, God had Job's vindication in mind from the beginning. Likewise, God had a plan to vindicate the woman with the issue of blood. This poor woman, who church history tells us was named Veronica, had been bleeding for twelve years. Veronica had been to every doctor she could find for help. They gladly took her money but offered her no healing breakthrough.

Veronica was so desperate for healing and so sure Jesus could vindicate her that she sought Him out as He walked through her town. Keep in mind that stoning was the penalty for a woman coming out in public while hemorrhaging. But after so many years of suffering physical issues as well as financial loss, Veronica decided to take her chances on Christ the healer. We read the account in Luke 8:43–48 (AMP):

> And a woman who had [suffered from] a hemorrhage for twelve years [and had spent all her money on physicians], and could not be healed by anyone, came up behind Him and touched the fringe of His outer robe, and immediately her bleeding stopped. Jesus said, "Who touched Me?"
>
> While they all were denying it, Peter [and those who were with him] said, "Master, the people are crowding and pushing against You!" But Jesus said, "Someone did touch Me, because I was aware that power [to heal] had gone out of Me."
>
> When the woman saw that she had not escaped notice, she came up trembling and fell down before Him. She declared in the presence of all the people the reason why she had touched Him, and how she had been immediately healed. He said to her, "Daughter, your faith [your personal trust and confidence in Me] has made you well. Go in peace (untroubled, undisturbed well-being)."

Veronica had risky faith—and her faith was rewarded after twelve years of suffering. We don't know how long

Job suffered, but some say it was two years. No matter how long you've been suffering in your body—or your emotions—know that there is healing vindication for you. Don't give up on God's promise.

CHAPTER 21

TILL DEATH DO US PART

THE PROPHET HOSEA married a prolific prostitute, knowing some of her children would be born from another man during their wedlock. Hosea wasn't compromising because he was head over heels in love with the call girl. He took Gomer as his wife because God commanded it.

God was trying to paint a picture. Hosea's puzzling marriage served as a parabolic message to Israel. The unlikely union between the holy prophet and the harlot was a metaphor for God's love for unfaithful Israel, a nation He delivered over and over again despite her offensive decision to chase after idols.

Hosea obeyed the word of the Lord and married Gomer. The newlyweds settled down and had three children together. Then, suddenly, without warning, Gomer abandoned her fledgling family. Having experienced spousal abandonment, I can imagine Hosea's pain. He loved her well, and she didn't even have the decency to leave him a note.

Sometime after Gomer went astray, God gave Hosea another hard-to-bear instruction:

> Then the LORD said to me, "Go and love your wife again, even though she commits adultery with another lover. This will illustrate that the LORD still loves Israel, even though the people have turned to other gods and love to worship them."
>
> So I bought her back for fifteen pieces of silver, five bushels of barley and a measure of wine. Then I said to her, "You must live in my house for many days and stop your prostitution. During this time, you will not have sexual relations with anyone, not even with me."
>
> —HOSEA 3:1–3, NLT

Many men would not even consider reuniting with a wayward wife after she left the family to fornicate for financial gain, but Hosea had the word of the Lord. Hosea saw Gomer through God's eyes.

Your spouse may not abandon the family and commit adultery like Gomer did, but make no mistake—you *will* face challenges in your marriage. To put it plainly, the enemy will launch assaults against your union in one or more of many ways. Remember, whether it's a human error or an enemy attack, God can and wants to bring vindication in your marriage.

WHY THE ENEMY HATES MARRIAGE

After God took a rib from Adam's sleeping body to create woman, Scripture reveals, "Therefore a man shall leave his father and mother and be joined to his wife, and they shall become one flesh" (Gen. 2:24). Almost immediately after they were joined together, Satan came to divide them. In Genesis 3, the snake in the Garden of Eden is lying to Adam's new bride. Satan's plan for division between man and wife didn't work in the Garden, but it has worked in many marriages since. The enemy hates marriage for many reasons.

Throughout Scripture, God uses marriage as an analogy for His love toward us. Jesus is the Bridegroom, and we are the bride. By inspiration of the Holy Spirit, Paul instructed men to love their wives as Christ loved the church and gave Himself up for her (Eph. 5:25) and that "husbands ought to love their wives as their own bodies" and "he who loves his wife loves himself" (Eph. 2:8). That is a self-sacrificial love, to be sure. Likewise, women are supposed to submit to their husbands in love.

But it's not always easy, especially with the accusing, thieving, destroying adversary on the scene. Satan hates marriage because he hates God. He hates God's plan. He doesn't want to see God's will done in the earth. He knows the power of a godly family to be a witness of His goodness and blessings. He attacks godly marriages, in particular, because divorce is not a good witness of God's reconciliatory power. And he wants to bring souls into grief and children into sorrow through broken homes.

Even if you are not married—whether you are single or divorced—you need to understand the importance of marriage to God's plan. God has a purpose for marriage, primarily to demonstrate His covenant but also for companionship, enjoyment, procreation, and protection. God established marriage because "it is not good for the man to be alone" (Gen. 2:18, NIV). We were created for love. Satan is hateful.

DISCERNING THE ENEMY

The enemy creeps into marriages in subtle ways. Distrust, disunity, financial disagreements, domestic violence, and addictions can destroy the covenant relationship. Neglect is the enemy's more subtle strategy to destabilize and destroy marriages. Perhaps the husband or the wife—or maybe both—are busy building their careers. Or maybe the desire to maintain relationships with old friends robs their spouses of much-needed affection. Neglecting your spouse, even if due to focusing on your children, can open the door to the enemy.

Envy and strife open a wide door for the enemy in your marriage. James 3:16 makes this abundantly clear: "For where envying and strife is, there is confusion and every evil work." Envy, jealousy, and strife are works of the flesh, but toxic emotions like anger, selfishness, and blame can also wreak havoc on your marriage.

Of course, there are more damaging sins, such as the adultery Hosea had to navigate. Nothing can ruin a marriage faster than a cheating spouse. The enemy will tempt married people to seek emotional understanding or physical satisfaction outside the marriage bed—through adultery or pornography—if they can't find it at home. And, of course, you've heard of emotional affairs. Cultivating healthy emotional and sexual connections with your spouse is critical.

Ultimately, many of these schisms the enemy introduces into marriage are rooted in prayerlessness. There's something to be said for the adage, "The couple that prays together stays together." Marriage is not easy, and

Satan knows that. He comes at opportune times to divide and conquer.

VINDICATION IN YOUR MARRIAGE

God hates divorce because of the pain it causes everyone involved—not just the husband and wife, but children and other family members. Whether your marriage is on the rocks or you are separated—or even if you are divorced—God can bring vindication to your marriage. This always starts with forgiveness. God can't restore a relationship where one person won't let go of offenses.

But if you are willing to forgive, you are positioning yourself for a stronger-than-ever marriage. You can have a fresh start, a new beginning. You can find yourself more in love than you ever have been. You can get that second chance, renew your vows, and learn to honor one another.

If the enemy has attacked your marriage, remind yourself of what made you fall in love with your spouse in the first place. Ask the Holy Spirit to show you the root of the problem, own your part, and make every effort to return to your first love. Talk it out with respect and true listening and find ways to connect again. Get counseling if you need it. More than anything, though, pray and declare God's will over your marriage. If God restored Gomer and Hosea, then He can restore your marriage.

PROPHESY TO THE DRY BONES

You may have to fight for the marriage, even if you are the only one fighting. You can stand against the enemy in the name of Jesus. God can cause those dry bones of your marriage to live again. Prophesy to the dry bones, like Ezekiel. Let Ezekiel 37:4–10 inspire you!

> Then he said to me, "Speak a prophetic message to these bones and say, 'Dry bones, listen to the word of the LORD! This is what the Sovereign LORD says: Look! I am going to put breath into you and make you live again! I will put flesh and muscles on you and cover you with skin. I will put breath into you, and you will come to life. Then you will know that I am the LORD.'"
>
> So I spoke this message, just as he told me. Suddenly as I spoke, there was a rattling noise all across the valley. The bones of each body came together and attached themselves as complete skeletons. Then as I watched, muscles and flesh formed over the bones. Then skin formed to cover their bodies, but they still had no breath in them.
>
> Then he said to me, "Speak a prophetic message to the winds, son of man. Speak a prophetic message and say, 'This is what the Sovereign LORD says: Come, O breath, from the four winds! Breathe into these dead bodies so they may live again.' So I spoke the message as he commanded me, and breath came into their bodies. They all came to life and stood up on their feet—a great army."

Speak life into your marriage and expect God to vindicate your union. Even if He doesn't—even if you cannot reconcile—you have sown sincere seed by faith, and God will take what the enemy meant for harm and turn it for your good. (See Genesis 50:20.)

CHAPTER 22

OVERUSED AND OVERLOOKED

W HEN I WAS a freelance writer, I ranked in the top 1 percent of income earners in my field. It wasn't because I was the best writer in the world. It was because I went the extra mile. I wrote, rewrote, and revised my copy before the editor ever laid eyes on it. I filed my stories before the deadline. I was willing to take the assignments no one else wanted and pinch-hit for other writers when they were sick or dropped the ball.

Indeed, I had a reputation for helping my editors clean up messes. But nobody likes to be used, abused—and then accused. So when the charge of envy was leveled against me because I suggested the editor was not qualified for her position (I was rewriting her cover stories on my own time every weekend), I felt more than a little slighted.

It reminded me of my college newspaper days when I was serving as managing editor. Week after week, the editor-in-chief failed to complete her duties. Week after week, I was up all night putting the newspaper to bed while she was out with friends or home in her own bed.

After about six months of carrying her load and mine, my grades started suffering.

Finally, I worked up the nerve to confront the situation. I told the newspaper adviser it wasn't right that she carried the editor role if she wasn't going to fulfill the editor's responsibilities. His reply: she's trying to get a journalism scholarship and needs the editorship on her résumé. My jaw dropped! I made it clear to my beloved adviser that I would not do the editor's job for her. I would resign, I told him, rather than let my grades suffer. He all but dared me to walk out the door.

GOD SEES YOUR HARD WORK

In both cases, God saw my hard work and vindicated me. I quit the student paper, even though I loved it, on principle. My fiancé was the chief photographer and followed me out the door. So did several of my friends on staff who saw the double standard. We started a paper and called it *The Independent*.

The first issue of our alternative school newspaper was a smashing success. The college president told us our paper was better than the official school paper and encouraged us to continue. He even urged us to apply for a grant. That made it all worth it. (The editor did get that scholarship but never had a journalism career.)

What about the magazine publisher who charged me with envy when I grew weary of rewriting the chief editor's stories every weekend? Suddenly the publisher had a revelation and decided he was wrong. The publisher fired the editor and offered me the position. And catch this, the role demanded a college degree—and I never finished college because I got married and had a baby. That's vindication!

WORK AS UNTO THE LORD

Maybe you've never been duped into doing someone else's work without compensation. Maybe your coworkers took credit for the stellar work you completed—or ideas you came up with. Maybe your boss is toxic and persecutes you, overlooking you for promotions you deserve and rejecting your requests for raises or even vacation time. Maybe your coworkers lie to you or about you. Maybe you can't trust anyone around you. I've been there—and so have many others.

I was saddened to learn nearly half of Black women in the UK working in professional jobs believe there will be times during their careers when they will be overlooked for promotions they are qualified for, according to a poll from Black Women in Leadership.[1] And about 90 percent of four hundred CEOs surveyed in 2023 said they'd be more likely to give in-person employees raises, promotions, or better assignments.[2] The workplace is not always a fair place.

So how do you tap into vindication in the workplace? First, get the right perspective. Remember who you are serving. Paul offered this sound advice: "And whatever you do, do it heartily, as to the Lord and not to men, knowing that from the Lord you will receive the reward of the inheritance; for you serve the Lord Christ" (Col. 3:23–24).

Paul wasn't being glib or offering platitudes. He was speaking from experience. As a tentmaker and preacher,

Paul understood what it was like to be persecuted doing his work. He explained to the church at Corinth: "And we labor, working with our own hands. Being reviled, we bless; being persecuted, we endure" (1 Cor. 4:12).

Solomon offered this parallel wisdom: "Whatever your hand finds to do, do it with your might; for there is no work or device or knowledge or wisdom in the grave where you are going" (Eccles. 9:10). And again, "In all labor there is profit" (Prov. 14:23). And again, "Do you see a man who excels in his work? He will stand before kings; he will not stand before unknown men" (Prov. 22:29).

LET GOD WORK ON YOUR HEART

And one more thing: while working in unpleasant circumstances, let God work on your heart and character. Joseph had two prophetic dreams that sent him into thirteen years of preparation to become prime minister of Egypt. God was working on his character so he would be fit to rule an empire. Joseph went through the wringer, so to speak.

First, Joseph had to endure sexual harassment in the workplace when Potiphar's wife made advances toward him—and then falsely accused him of trying to rape her. Next, Joseph was sent to prison, where God gave him favor and stewardship over the entire campus. But he was more concerned with getting out of jail than getting the character flaws out of his soul. When he interpreted the dreams of the baker and the butler accurately, he pled, "Remember me when it is well with you, and please show kindness to me; make mention of me to Pharaoh, and get me out of this house" (Gen. 40:14).

God was working on Joseph, and He may be working on you. If you were ready to handle the promotion now, God would give it to you now. Many times, we need to develop the character that will keep us where the anointing takes us. Romans 5:3–5 tells us patience produces character. Ask the Holy Spirit to show you areas of your life that need work—and then ask Him for the grace to get to the next glory.

Remember, humility has no rights. Here are three witnesses to keep in mind: "Humble yourselves under the mighty hand of God, that He may exalt you in due time" (1 Pet. 5:6–7); "Humble yourselves in the sight of the Lord, and He will lift you up" (Jas. 4:10); and, "Whoever exalts himself will be humbled, and he who humbles himself will be exalted" (Luke 14:11). If you need vindication in your career, wait on the Lord and walk humbly.

CHAPTER 23

GENERATIONAL VINDICATION

JABEZ WAS CURSED on the day he was born—by his mother! She was not an evil woman who never wanted to be pregnant and regretted having a baby. In fact, she goes down in biblical history as a godly mother who raised her son to walk in honor, walk with Jehovah, and walk by faith. Nevertheless, the enemy inspired this godly woman to curse her son after the anguish of childbirth—and if that curse hadn't been broken, it could have plagued Jabez's bloodline.

How did Jabez's mother curse him? Quite unintentionally. She cursed her newborn son when she named him Jabez, which means "sorrow" or "one who causes pain." The young mother wasted no time blaming her bouncing baby boy for the agony she experienced bringing him into the world. Doubtless, she didn't consider the long-term consequences of her words. Jabez was stigmatized and set up to be a failure, marked as one who causes sorrow. Think about it. Whenever someone called out to him, "Jabez!" they essentially said, "Hey, One Who Causes Pain." It would be like your parents naming you Disaster or Problematic. That's hard on the self-esteem.

Jabez could have lived his whole life under the dark cloud of that spontaneous curse and allowed its effects to harass his future generations. But Jabez understood the goodness of God. Jabez didn't settle for the curse. He extended his faith for the blessing. In 1 Chronicles 4:10, he launched out in prayer with three words that started changing the trajectory of his life, "Bless me indeed."

Understand the power of the Hebrew word *indeed*. It means "without any question: truly, undeniably; often used interjectionally to express irony or disbelief or surprise."[1] Jabez's mother had cursed him. Everyone who called his name was cursing him day by day. But man's curse does not overrule God's blessing. Jabez prayed a simple prayer, "'Oh, that You would bless me indeed, and enlarge my territory, that Your hand would be with me, and that You would keep me from evil, that I may not cause pain!' So God granted him what he requested" (1 Chron. 4:10).

With that simple prayer, Jabez turned what would have been a generational curse into a generational vindication. Though the enemy had a plan for his bloodline and activated it the day he was born through his mother's ignorance, Jabez understood the power of God's grace and essentially asked Him to turn the curse into a blessing (Deut. 23:5). He did it for Jabez, and He can do it for you.

When the generational curse is broken, the stage is set for generational blessings—and generational vindication. Maybe everyone in your family line has been afflicted with poverty, addiction, or depression. Maybe your DNA seems to be marked with failure and setbacks. Maybe you are serving the Lord with your whole heart, but cycles of betrayal, sickness, and disease have rippled through your family tree. God wants to break the generational curse and give you generational vindication through blessings that make you rich, joyful, healed, and whole—without sorrow.

GENERATIONAL BLESSINGS ABOUND

Generational blessings are valid. We see the concept throughout Scripture. If you meditate on what the Word says about generational blessings, you can build your faith case for generational vindication—and not just for you but also for your children and their children's children and their children's children's children.

The Psalms are a strategic place to start. Psalm 145:4 tells us: "One generation shall praise Your works to another, and shall declare Your mighty acts." Psalm 100:5 promises: "For the LORD is good; His mercy is everlasting, and His truth endures to all generations."

Psalm 119:90 reveals: "Your faithfulness endures to all generations; You established the earth, and it abides." And Psalm 112:2 tells us: "His descendants will be mighty on earth; the generation of the upright will be blessed." And Psalm 71:18 insists: "Now also when I am old and gray-headed, O God, do not forsake me, until I declare Your strength to this generation, your power to everyone who is to come."

Of course, there are conditions for generational vindication. We must break the curses and keep declaring His mighty acts even when the enemy's curses are visibly working against us. We need to keep speaking the truth that sets us free until we see the full measure of freedom Jesus died to give us. We need to believe He is faithful to watch over the word He has spoken into our lives (Jer. 1:12).

We need to cooperate with the grace of Elohim and seek first the kingdom of God and His righteousness so the generational blessings will chase down and overtake the damage generational curses have brought into our lives. God wants us to declare His strength and power instead of focusing on the strong attack and the power of the enemy that is manifesting in our lives. The blood speaks a better word!

WALKING IN GENERATIONAL BLESSINGS

Paul understood the psalmist's declarations and saw the generational blessing working in his spiritual son Timothy's life. Those blessings encouraged Paul on his journeys. We read in 2 Timothy 1:5: "When I call to remembrance the genuine faith that is in you, which dwelt first in your grandmother Lois and your mother Eunice, and I am persuaded is in you also."

Maybe you don't have a heritage of faith to tap into. Maybe you are the first in your bloodline to put faith in Christ. Maybe you are the first to pursue the ultimate generational vindication that is found in Him. That means you are the forerunner of Genesis 22:18, in which God spoke to Abraham: "In your seed all the nations of the earth shall be blessed, because you have obeyed My voice."

Christ is Abraham's seed. The blessed Son of God dwells in you. He is the hope of glory (Col. 1:27). He is the hope of vindication—even generational vindication.

That means you can claim this vindication for your family, even before they are born. You can declare, "And His mercy is on those who fear Him from generation to generation" (Luke 1:50). You can stand on Deuteronomy 7:9, "Therefore know that the Lord your God, He is God, the faithful God who keeps covenant and mercy for a thousand generations with those who love Him and keep His commandments."

CHAPTER 24

VINDICATED BY ANGELS

W HEN I WROTE *Angels on Assignment Again*, I went on an "angel hunt" in Scripture. I studied every minute detail concerning angels and was struck by these heavenly beings' diverse roles and functions. Yes, angels are messengers sent to minister to the heirs of salvation (Heb. 1:14). But angels are not confined to a faster-than-the-speed-of-light message delivery service. Angels have a wide variety of divine assignments, from comforting and strengthening God's people to helping interpret dreams to rebuke. (I'd hate to have an angel rebuke me!)

Years after I wrote the book, God showed me another aspect of angelic ministry: angels of vindication. Yes, God can choose to send angels to help bring forth your vindication. Remember, Psalm 103:20 puts it plainly, "Bless the LORD, you His angels, who excel in strength, who do His word, heeding the voice of His word." When you are wronged, put to shame, misjudged, or face injustice of any kind, God's word over your life is vindication. That's His promise—and Jesus understood this.

When the Roman soldiers came to arrest Jesus after He had surrendered His will to the Father in the Garden of Gethsemane, He pointed to vindicating angels: "And suddenly, one of those who were with Jesus stretched out his hand and drew his sword, struck the servant of the high priest, and cut off his ear. But Jesus said to him, 'Put your sword in its place, for all who take the sword will perish by the sword. Or do you think that I cannot now pray to My Father, and He will provide Me with more than twelve legions of angels?'" (Matt. 26:51–53). Did you see it?

ANGELS VINDICATED MARY

Angels vindicated Mary, the mother of Jesus, in a spectacular way. To be sure, it would have to take a dramatic encounter for any man to accept an "immaculate conception" that left his fiancée suddenly pregnant. If angels hadn't come to vindicate her, Mary's storyline may have turned out quite different. Let's look at the whole account in Matthew 1:18–25:

> Now the birth of Jesus Christ was as follows: After His mother Mary was betrothed to Joseph, before they came together, she was found with child of the Holy Spirit. Then Joseph her husband, being a just man, and not wanting to make her a public example, was minded to put her away secretly.
>
> But while he thought about these things, behold, an angel of the Lord appeared to him in a dream, saying, "Joseph, son of David, do not be afraid to take to you Mary your wife, for that which is conceived in her is of the Holy Spirit. And she will bring forth a Son, and you shall call His name JESUS, for He will save His people from their sins."
>
> So all this was done that it might be fulfilled

which was spoken by the Lord through the prophet, saying: "Behold, the virgin shall be with child, and bear a Son, and they shall call His name Immanuel," which is translated, "God with us." Then Joseph, being aroused from sleep, did as the angel of the Lord commanded him and took to him his wife, and did not know her till she had brought forth her firstborn Son. And he called His name Jesus.

Angels can visit people in their dreams to vindicate you. Angels can likewise appear to people in visions to vindicate you. This is a dazzling form of vindication that we don't see every day. But there are times when God, in His sovereignty, decides angelic vindication is the best way to get someone's attention.

ANGELS VINDICATED A PROPHET

Angels vindicated the prophet Daniel. The prophet had favor with Darius, the reigning king in Babylon. Babylonian officials were jealous of Daniel because he outranked many of them in authority. In their jealousy, the crafty Babylonians looked for ways to remove Daniel from his post.

You know the story: These wicked servants tricked Darius into signing a decree that stated no one in the land could petition any god or man for thirty days except the king. It sounded reasonable to Darius, so he signed the decree without considering how it might impact Daniel.

Unbeknownst to Darius, his signature unleashed what could have been deadly warfare against the prophet. Despite his knowledge of the decree, Daniel's passion for

God compelled him to open his windows and pray three times a day without fear of who would see him.

Daniel was soon thrown into a lion's den, and a stone secured the entryway. There was no natural way of escape! When Darius heard about the setup, he fasted and prayed for Daniel, his trusted adviser, all night. The next morning, he ran to the lion's den to see what happened to Daniel. No one could have expected it, but he was vindicated by angels. Daniel said: "My God sent His angel and shut the lions' mouths, so that they have not hurt me, because I was found innocent before Him; and also, O king, I have done no wrong before you" (Dan. 6:22).

Darius called Daniel out of the den and threw in the wicked servants—and their wives and children—who had manipulated him into signing a death warrant against Daniel. Then Darius signed a decree that everyone must tremble before Daniel's God. That's angelic vindication! Now consider Hezekiah's testimony.

ANGELS VINDICATED A KING

Hezekiah was one of Israel's righteous kings. His reign started when he was only twenty-five years old, and "he did what was right in the sight of the LORD, according to all that his father David had done" (2 Kings 18:3). That's high praise considering David was known as a man after God's own heart. Hezekiah tore down idols in the land, and revival hit Israel.

Revival was in the air until the day Assyria's king attacked Israel and took her land. Later, Assyria also took Judah. Hezekiah tried to make peace with the enemy king. He paid three hundred thousand talents of silver

and thirty talents of gold—basically everything he had—
as a ransom for Israel and Judah. But silver and gold
didn't satisfy the wicked king. Instead, he tightened the
screws on Israel.

Hezekiah was beside himself. A messenger from the
enemy tried to publicly disgrace Hezekiah in front of his
staff, ridiculing him for trusting in the Lord for deliverance. (Bad move!) The messenger tried to turn God's
people against Hezekiah with false promises of prosperity
and security under Assyrian rule. Hezekiah called it a
day of trouble, rebuke, and blasphemy (2 Kings 19:3). His
faithful servants ran to Isaiah the prophet for help. Isaiah
prophesied:

> Thus you shall say to your master, "Thus says the
> LORD: 'Do not be afraid of the words which you
> have heard, with which the servants of the king of
> Assyria have blasphemed Me. Surely I will send
> a spirit upon him, and he shall hear a rumor and
> return to his own land; and I will cause him to fall
> by the sword in his own land.'"
>
> —2 KINGS 19:6–7

The drama continued to unfold with the Assyrians
spewing threats. Finally, the enemy sent a letter to
Hezekiah that brought him to his knees in prayer. That
prayer led to a lengthy prophecy from Isaiah that promised victory over the king of Assyria. God decided to
fight this battle for the righteous king. God decided to
vindicate Hezekiah through the ministry of angels.

Second Kings 19:35 offers the story: "And it came to
pass on a certain night that the angel of the LORD went

out, and killed in the camp of the Assyrians one hundred and eighty-five thousand; and when people arose early in the morning, there were the corpses—all dead." Now that's vindication!

CHAPTER 25

VINDICATION IN THE COURTS OF HEAVEN

I T WAS THE first time I had ever entered the courts of heaven—and it was a last resort. I was desperate for vindication after a once-dear friend went on a warpath against me because God told me to draw back from the relationship. Clearly, she was hurt even though she should have seen it coming because she had started slowly pulling away months earlier.

When I shared the Lord's direction for me to move in a different direction and cut some partnerships, she wrote me vicious letters, made nasty accusations behind my back, went on a social media tirade against me, and rallied as many others to her side as she could. Her smear campaign rippled through our social circles. All the while, I was biting my tongue.

I understood she was hurt and that hurting people hurt people, but she had more than crossed a line. She was publicly sharing sensitive personal information I disclosed to her in private. She was also calling conference hosts with whom I was scheduled to speak and spewing wicked words that caused them to cancel at the last minute. That led to a financial hit on top of relational hits. I was losing

friends who took her side, and I was losing opportunities across the board. She even spread rumors about me
among my mentors.

After exhausting all possibilities to calm the raging
fire her tongue ignited against me, I took my case to the
courts of heaven. I prayed God would show her mercy
and asked for justice. Things soon settled down for me.
Opportunities came back around. Finances were restored,
but it didn't go as well for her.

Because she would not repent—and had treated at least
half a dozen people the same way she treated me—this
woman soon saw people leaving her ministry in droves,
citing toxic control. Her daughter was exposed in a major
sex scandal. She too was accused of sexual sin and was
under immense financial pressure. I am not saying God
judged her. I am saying she reaped a harvest on the
wicked seeds she sowed because she would not repent.
She opened the door to the enemy. Remember, I had
prayed mercy on her. It was hard to watch.

SELECTIVE COURT DATES

I'm not one who runs to the courts of heaven for anything
and everything. I don't believe it's necessary or even wise
to do so any more than it's necessary or wise to run to
a natural court of law for every dispute that occurs. But
there have been a few times I've sought vindication from
the courts of heaven. There have been times when the
Holy Spirit led me to plead my case to the judge who sits
on the throne.

This is scriptural. In Luke's Gospel, Jesus offers the
parable of the persistent widow. The parable features a

widow going before a judge. You may have read this passage many times without reading it through this lens, which compares an unjust judge on the earth to a righteous judge seated on a heavenly throne. Luke 18:1–8 lays it out:

> Then He spoke a parable to them, that men always ought to pray and not lose heart, saying: "There was in a certain city a judge who did not fear God nor regard man. Now there was a widow in that city; and she came to him, saying, 'Get justice for me from my adversary.' And he would not for a while; but afterward he said within himself, 'Though I do not fear God nor regard man, yet because this widow troubles me I will avenge her, lest by her continual coming she weary me.'"
>
> Then the Lord said, "Hear what the unjust judge said. And shall God not avenge His own elect who cry out day and night to Him, though He bears long with them? I tell you that He will avenge them speedily. Nevertheless, when the Son of Man comes, will He really find faith on the earth?"

WHO'S YOUR JUDGE?

Notice here the unjust judge. Maybe you've been judged unjustly. Maybe natural court cases have been ruled in favor of the one who wronged you. Maybe the enemy of your soul has condemned you over past mistakes. But your judge is also your Bridegroom and King. Your judge is the Creator of the universe. Your judge is a just judge.

Maybe people have defied Scripture and passed judgment on you because of your race, your age, your education, or your personality. Maybe you've been judged based on your physical appearance, hair, or clothing. Maybe the religious system has judged you as inadequate to pursue your high calling because you are a woman or divorced or didn't graduate from the right seminary. The world and the church are not your judge. Your boss is not your judge. Your neighbor is not your judge. God is your judge. And your judge is your vindicator.

You are a servant of the Most High God. When Paul the apostle said, "Who are you to judge another's servant? To his own master he stands or falls. Indeed, he will be made to stand, for God is able to make him stand" (Rom. 14:4). And James put it this way: "There is one Lawgiver, who is able to save and to destroy. Who are you to judge another?" (James 4:12).

God is a righteous judge and is for you, not against you. When you've been wronged, there are times when the Holy Spirit will lead you to the courtroom of heaven to deal with the matter. If the persistent widow could get a just verdict from an unjust judge, surely we can get a just verdict from our loving judge.

APPROACHING GOD AS JUDGE

You approach God as a judge in a different way than you approach Him as a healer or deliverer. First, we must remember that God is the "Judge of all" (Heb. 12:23). God sees everything everyone did to you, but He also sees your flaws and shortcomings. If we have unforgiveness and bitterness in our hearts toward the one who wronged us, then we won't find vindication from the judge. We'll find conviction from the Holy Spirit.

Before you approach the courts of heaven, examine your heart. Repent for any unforgiveness, wrong attitudes, or vengeance you're harboring. The judge won't hear your case until you do. Thankfully, it's easy to meet His conditions. If you confess your sins, He is faithful and just to forgive your sin and cleanse you from all unrighteousness (1 John 1:9). Forgive from your heart and let it go, so you can receive vindication.

With clean hands and a pure heart, you can approach the judge with reverential fear. Just as in the natural court, lawyers call the judge "Your honor," you must have a heart posture of honor for God and His Word on which you stand for vindication. The one who wronged you was not operating in the fear of the Lord, but you must. Solomon assured us, "In the fear of the LORD there is strong confidence, and His children will have a place of refuge" (Prov. 14:26).

DAVID'S PRAYER IN THE COURTS OF HEAVEN

Entire book series have been written about operating in the courts of heaven—and there's no lack of "suggestions" online about how to pray in this dimension. But take caution. Some have taken the courts of heaven revelation into a ditch of extremes.

For the sake of balance and biblical accuracy in our heart's cry for vindication, we can use the model prayer David penned, a psalm that appeals to the judge's heart. It's Psalm 35, which is David's heartfelt prayer to the Lord as avenger.

Plead my cause, O LORD, with those who strive with me; fight against those who fight against me. Take hold of shield and buckler, and stand up for my help. Also draw out the spear, and stop those who pursue me. Say to my soul, "I am your salvation."

Let those be put to shame and brought to dishonor who seek after my life; let those be turned back and brought to confusion who plot my hurt. Let them be like chaff before the wind, and let the angel of the LORD chase them. Let their way be dark and slippery, and let the angel of the LORD pursue them. For without cause they have hidden their net for me in a pit, which they have dug without cause for my life. Let destruction come upon him unexpectedly, and let his net that he has hidden catch himself; into that very destruction let him fall.

And my soul shall be joyful in the LORD; it shall rejoice in His salvation. All my bones shall say, "LORD, who is like You, delivering the poor from him who is too strong for him, yes, the poor and the needy from him who plunders him?"

Fierce witnesses rise up; they ask me things that I do not know. They reward me evil for good, to the sorrow of my soul. But as for me, when they were sick, my clothing was sackcloth; I humbled myself with fasting; and my prayer would return to my own heart. I paced about as though he were my friend or brother; I bowed down heavily, as one who mourns for his mother.

But in my adversity they rejoiced and gathered together; attackers gathered against me, and I did not know it; they tore at me and did not cease; with ungodly mockers at feasts they gnashed at me with their teeth. Lord, how long will You look on? Rescue me from their destructions, my precious life from the lions. I will give You thanks in the great assembly; I will praise You among many people.

Let them not rejoice over me who are wrongfully my enemies; nor let them wink with the eye who hate me without a cause. For they do not speak peace, but they devise deceitful matters against the quiet ones in the land. They also opened their mouth wide against me, and said, "Aha, aha! Our eyes have seen it."

This You have seen, O Lord; do not keep silence. O Lord, do not be far from me. Stir up Yourself, and awake to my vindication, to my cause, my God and my Lord. Vindicate me, O Lord my God, according to Your righteousness; and let them not rejoice over me. Let them not say in their hearts, "Ah, so we would have it!" Let them not say, "We have swallowed him up."

Let them be ashamed and brought to mutual confusion who rejoice at my hurt; let them be clothed with shame and dishonor who exalt themselves against me. Let them shout for joy and be glad, who favor my righteous cause; and let them say continually, "Let the Lord be magnified, who has pleasure in the prosperity of His servant.'" And my tongue shall speak of Your righteousness and of Your praise all the day long.

I have an entire course on www.schoolofthespirit.tv called "Getting Justice in the Courts of Heaven." This course offers an in-depth look at how to approach the courts of heaven for vindication.

CHAPTER 26

WHILE YOU WAIT

I DIDN'T JUST GET saved in jail—I got radically saved in jail. When I got out on the fortieth day, I actively searched for opportunities to serve the One who saved my life. I was a journalist, so I saw writing as a natural expression of my devotion. The only problem was I didn't yet have enough of the Word in my heart to properly advance His cause.

I set out to learn the Word of God and soon became an avid Joyce Meyer follower. I signed up as a volunteer usher at the conference when I heard she was coming to a city near me. I didn't know it when I signed up—I was just serving unto the Lord—but it was a pre-vindication setup.

Joyce was talking about God as our vindicator. That message was music to my ears because I still desperately needed God's vindication on many fronts. Despite my miraculous vindication and release from a ten-year prison sentence, there were still many wrongs that only God could make right.

First off, most of my family turned against me when I decided to follow Jesus. My parents especially weren't thrilled with my "jailhouse religion" or my plans to move

six hundred miles away to escape the worldly associa-
tions of my past and start a new life in Christ. Hoping
to change my made-up mind, my parents issued a threat:
if you leave Florida, you can't take the car we gave you.
(They gave me their old car some years earlier when my
grandmother gave them a brand-new one.) Even worse,
my grandmother—the same grandmother who helped me
escape the prison sentence—announced she was starting
a prayer chain to stop me from moving.

It was beyond hurtful. I was still walking through the
aftermath of a major trial—my husband had abandoned
the family, I spent forty days in jail, and I had lost my
life's savings and my career. All I wanted was a fresh start,
and the people who were supposed to stand with me were
standing against me. I was prepared to go without a car
and a family blessing because I had the word of the Lord
to move. I trusted Him to find a way even when it didn't
look like there was a way. So I prayed my simple "Help
me, God" prayer and waited on the Lord.

A week hadn't passed when my grandma called me to
apologize. She told me she didn't want me to move so
far away, but the Lord showed her I was making the best
decision for my future. The Lord also told her to help
me. My grandmother immediately called my parents and
let them know if they took away my car, she would take
away the car she gave them. I was shocked, but it was
justice.

Unfortunately, my car conked out on the road in
the middle of nowhere a few months later. My parents
weren't talking to me. I had no money. I had no credit.
I didn't know what to do. That's when Grandma came

to the rescue again. Grandpa called me and offered to cosign for a brand-new vehicle. Within a week, I was back on my feet. It was not only the vindication of God but the provision of God. Nothing is too hard for God! (See Jeremiah 32:17.)

Vindication seemed to come swiftly and payback promptly when I was a baby Christian. As I started growing up in Christ, I had to learn to wait on Him as the voice of injustice was screaming, "Take matters into your own hands!" in the wake of injustice. More than once, I've had to wait years upon years for God to show up as my vindicator. I want to encourage you to wait on God for your vindication. No matter how long it takes for your vindication, I promise it will be worth it.

LET YOUR HEART TAKE COURAGE

When you wait patiently on the Lord for vindication, you gain courage in the process. David said in Psalm 27:13–14, "I would have lost heart, unless I had believed that I would see the goodness of the LORD in the land of the living. Wait on the LORD; be of good courage, and He shall strengthen your heart; wait, I say, on the LORD!"

Keep in mind this was David's declaration of faith at a time in his life when everything seemed dark. David had been anointed king of Israel, but the current king, Saul, was hunting him down like a dog with a mind to kill him. Saul positioned David as the enemy even though the future king's intentions toward him were nothing but kind. David knew he couldn't take matters into his own hands and deal with Saul directly. He knew he had to wait on the Lord for vindication. Eventually, Saul died in battle, and David was installed as king.

David later wrote, "Our soul waits for the LORD; He is our help and our shield. For our heart shall rejoice in Him, because we have trusted in His holy name. Let Your mercy, O LORD, be upon us, just as we hope in You (Ps. 33:20–22). And again in Psalm 37:34 David continued to declare his decision to wait on the Lord for vindication despite the persecution, "Wait on the LORD, and keep His way, and He shall exalt you to inherit the land; when the wicked are cut off, you shall see it" (Ps. 37:34).

God is saying to you what He said to Joshua, "Have I not commanded you? Be strong and of good courage; do not be afraid, nor be dismayed, for the LORD your God is with you wherever you go" (Josh. 1:9). The Lord is with you when you wait. In fact, He's working things out behind the scenes while you wait in faith and trust. When you remind yourself of this truth, it will strengthen your resolve to wait for His vindication.

WAITING ON THE GOD OF JUSTICE

Isaiah understood Jesus as Bridegroom, King, and Judge. He once said, "Therefore the LORD will wait, that He may be gracious to you; and therefore He will be exalted, that He may have mercy on you. For the LORD is a God of justice; blessed are all those who wait for Him" (Isa. 30:18). Remember this: While you are waiting for the blessing of justice, you can find uncommon blessings in the waiting.

In other words, waiting on God comes with unique blessings. If you learn to wait on the Lord for your vindication—really wait on the Lord—you'll be doubly blessed in the practice. We grow in faith when we wait on the Lord. (See Hebrews 11:6.) We develop our spiritual ears to hear Him more clearly. We receive the grace we need to succeed. We gain the wisdom we need to prosper. (See 1 John 5:4.) We learn of His ways. We become more like Him as we spend that time with Him. Charles Spurgeon once wrote:

> Shall he forget you, when he clothes the grass of the field, and when he makes the valleys rejoice with food? But is your anxiety about your character? Has some one been slandering you? And are you troubled and grieved, lest you should lose your good name? If a man has called you every name in the world, do not go to law with him. "Wait only upon God."
>
> If you have been reviled in every newspaper and falsely charged in every sheet, never answer—leave it alone. "Vengeance is mine; I will repay, saith the Lord." Practise non-resistance in words, as well as in deeds. Just bow yourself, and let the missiles fly over your head. Stand not up to resist. To resist slander is to make it worse. The only way to blunt the edge of calumny [libel or defamation] is to be silent: it can do no hurt when we are still. Where no wood is the fire goeth out; and if you will not refute nor answer, the fire will die out of itself. Let it alone. "Wait thou only upon God."[1]

WHEN YOU ARE WEARY OF WAITING

Even with Scripture to lean on, the truth is waiting can get old. When you get weary of waiting, it means you aren't waiting on the Lord. You are waiting, but not on and with the Lord. You've somehow left Him out of the waiting equation. Isaiah 40:31 promises, "But those who wait on the LORD shall renew their strength; they shall mount up with wings like eagles, they shall run and not be weary, they shall walk and not faint."

If you feel like you just can't wait anymore, turn your attention to the Lord as you wait. When you do, He will renew your strength. When you feel weak, when you want to lash out at the one who wronged you, when the enemy is tempting your tongue to tell everyone what they did to you, when you want to vindicate yourself, intentionally wait on the Lord instead. Gaze upon His beauty. Meditate on His promises. When you do, God will strengthen your resolve and give you the grace to wait on His vindication.

But more than that, God will give you His perspective. You will rise above the situation and look down on the issue from His point of view. You'll see the injustice through a different lens. Remember, His ways are higher than our ways, and His thoughts are higher than our thoughts (Isa. 55:8-9). When you wait on Him, you learn His ways and tap into His thought process. You begin to understand what Joseph knew.

LIVE LIKE JOSEPH

After Jacob died, Joseph's brothers—who had sold him as a slave before he was falsely accused of rape and thrown into prison—were afraid he would take vengeance on them. They were scared because their father, Jacob, wasn't there to defend them. What they didn't know was that all those years of waiting on the Lord in prison prepared Joseph to take a different perspective. Genesis 50:15–21 tells us:

> When Joseph's brothers saw that their father was dead, they said, "Perhaps Joseph will hate us, and may actually repay us for all the evil which we did to him." So they sent messengers to Joseph, saying, "Before your father died he commanded, saying, 'Thus you shall say to Joseph: "I beg you, please forgive the trespass of your brothers and their sin; for they did evil to you."' Now, please, forgive the trespass of the servants of the God of your father."
>
> And Joseph wept when they spoke to him. Then his brothers also went and fell down before his face, and they said, "Behold, we are your servants."
>
> Joseph said to them, "Do not be afraid, for am I in the place of God? But as for you, you meant evil against me; but God meant it for good, in order to bring it about as it is this day, to save many people alive. Now therefore, do not be afraid; I will provide for you and your little ones." And he comforted them and spoke kindly to them.

Can you see it? Joseph knew God turned the enemy's plans for good. As you wait on Him, I pray you will get that revelation and it will help you wait patiently with a courageous heart, a forgiving heart, and a heart that's willing to bless even your enemies.

CHAPTER 27

YOUR KAIROS TIME

STAY CALM. BE patient. Your time is coming." I heard the Lord thunder those words at the point of my new beginning. Only days earlier, I was vindicated of a false accusation and released from jail after forty days of unjust incarceration that cost me nearly everything I had.

After I was freed from the bars that held me captive—both physically and spiritually—I was forced to move back in with my parents. Because my father expected me to go to prison for ten years, he gave up my apartment and gave away my dog. I had no money, dog, job, home—nothing in this natural world. (Sounds like a sad country song!) But I did have Christ. And He is always enough. And in Christ, I also had a promise of vindication. But the fullness of my vindication wasn't immediate, and the months following my dramatic salvation were difficult.

For starters, the economy was in shambles. Freelance writers were not in demand—and the only career path I knew was journalism. I had spent most of my money paying the defense attorney to overthrow the false charges, so I was essentially penniless. Newly born-again, I didn't know much of the Word of God, and I didn't know how to pray. My prayer life at that time consisted of, "Help me, God. Thank You, God."

AN ENCOUNTER WITH GOD

Late one night, after an especially difficult day, I went to the spare bedroom in my parents' house to pray. My daughter was sleeping across the hall, and my folks were asleep on the other side of the house. I knelt over a chair and began crying out to God for help.

I prayed so long I fell asleep with my head on the seat of the chair. Suddenly I awoke to the sound of a booming voice with a divine announcement: "Stay calm. Be patient. Your time is coming." Startled is not a strong enough word for my reaction to the midnight revelation. I looked all around me. I thought it was my dad, but it didn't sound like his voice. When I saw no one in the dark room, the spirit of the fear of the Lord fell upon me. I slowly got up and went to bed, pondering the incident half the night like Samuel after his first encounter with God.

I didn't know it at the time, but I had heard the audible voice of God. Some years later, I realized it was God Himself speaking words of life. Nevertheless, I stored those words in my heart for many years while I waited for my ultimate vindication.

CONTINUING TRIALS AND TRIBULATIONS

Getting out of jail wasn't the end of my trials and tribulations. In some ways, it was just the beginning. God put me on a fast track to perfecting my faith, and I experienced what felt like more than my fair share of suffering. I moved from my parents' house in Florida to Alabama to make a fresh start. The start wasn't so fresh. Some neighbors took advantage of me. Some supposed friends stole from me. I had barely enough money to get by and ended up on food stamps while I tried to rebuild my life.

During that time, I kept pondering God's words that were stored in my heart: "Stay calm. Be patient. Your time is coming." I didn't know how long I would have to stay calm, but I gradually learned to still my soul. I pressed into Philippians 4:6–7, "Be anxious for nothing, but in everything by prayer and supplication, with thanksgiving, let your requests be made known to God; and the peace of God, which surpasses all understanding, will guard your hearts and minds through Christ Jesus."

I didn't know how long I would have to be patient, but I learned that by faith and patience, we inherit the promises of God. (See Hebrews 6:12.) I didn't know when my time would come, but I believed it was coming so I pressed into Galatians 6:9, "And let us not grow weary while doing good, for in due season we shall reap if we do not lose heart."

MY KAIROS TIME ARRIVED

Finally, around 2011, my kairos time arrived. Before I tell you how that happened, it's important to understand the Greek word translated "season" in Galatians 6:9 is *kairos*. *Kairos* means "a fixed and definite time...the decisive epoch waited for, opportune or seasonable time," according to *The New Testament Greek Lexicon*.[1] *HELPS Word Studies* adds some additional insight. *Kairos* means "time as opportunity"; "derived from *kara* ('head') referring to things 'coming to a head' to take full-advantage of"; "the suitable time, the right moment...a favorable moment."[2]

Nearly a decade after the Lord said, "Stay calm. Be patient. Your time is coming," God spoke again. I was at home in worship when the Holy Spirit whispered four words to my heart that I had waited to hear for years: "This is your time." I immediately knew what He meant. I remembered leaning over that chair, praying in faith to a God I barely knew and couldn't see so many years earlier. I remembered Him speaking eight words at one of my life's lowest points. Ever since then, my life has been on a fast track of growth in every area. Sure, there are still trials and tribulations, but I'm in my time.

My kairos time hasn't ended. It started with vindication in the realm of book publishing. I had written and rewritten books for men of God who took advantage of my skills without so much as a kind word. When my time came, I suddenly started getting book deals from multiple publishers. I had labored long to produce television programs for preachers who, again, didn't care what their success cost me. Suddenly I started appearing on major Christian television shows. And it hasn't stopped. Vindication is the story of my life. Little by little, the Lord is repaying me.

DISCERNING YOUR KAIROS TIME

We need to be like the sons of Issachar, having an understanding of the times in our lives and in the world around us. (See 1 Chronicles 12:32.) The devils know their kairos time. The enemy knows his time is short, and that is why you may be experiencing so much warfare. Of course, there is more than one kairos time in your life.

So how do you discern your kairos time for vindication? Well, God could speak to you as He did me. He also could send an angel or a prophet to announce your kairos time. But barring these supernatural events, you can discern by paying attention to what's going on in your life. For example, you may sense a rumbling.

Before my kairos time for vindication manifested, I had been feeling a rumbling in my life for two years. I knew the winds of change were coming, but nothing vindication-worthy was happening. God was making new divine connections and disconnections. He was changing my natural and spiritual appetites, but there was no spectacular breakthrough moment, so to speak, for a long time. When you sense a rumbling, ask the Holy Spirit what's happening. He may or may not tell you, but being spiritually curious can yield the fruit of insight.

You can also think back to the prayers you prayed and the prophetic words spoken over your life to discern what God is about to do. When I considered the petitions I had made to God over the years, I started to see how He was answering. Ask yourself, "Are my prayers coming to pass in a different way than I imagined?" Sometimes we pray specific prayers and expect a specific answer—but sometimes God answers in a way we don't see coming. Vindication may look different than you thought.

What prophetic words released over your life—or other words the Holy Spirit has spoken to your heart—are pointing to the time you are entering? It's important to keep a record and review the prophecies spoken over your life so you can wait in faith for their manifestation. Most of the time, you have to wage war with them, according to 1 Timothy 1:18. God's will usually doesn't just happen without any action on our part. It needs to be bathed in prayer.

PREPARE FOR THE PROMISE

Once you sense your kairos time is near, start preparing to step into the fullness of the promise. What are you doing to prepare yourself spiritually, physically, relationally, and financially for that kairos moment of vindication? Do you need to forgive anyone? Do you need to cultivate new relationships?

Remember, you can't make a kairos moment happen— these are God-ordained times—but you can believe to enter into it. In fact, you need faith to enter into it. Know that God has a kairos time for you. He is not slack about His promises. He doesn't always fulfill His Word in our lives when we'd like Him to, but He does watch over His Word to perform it (Jer. 1:12). If He said it, and you believed it and prayed it through, it will happen in His timing.

Stay alert. Watch and pray. You can miss a kairos moment if you are not spiritually minded. Set your mind on things above instead of on the things of the earth

(Col. 3:2). Once you've discerned it's your kairos time, quickly get into agreement with God. Surrender your will to the Lord and hold on! Vindication has come to you.

CHAPTER 28

STANDING FOR DOUBLE VINDICATION

WHEN I SHARED what was one of the most unique book ideas I'd ever had with Alex, I had no idea he would go to my publisher, pitch it as his own thought, and sign a contract to write a book behind my back. It was disappointing, but his behavior after being exposed was jaw-dropping.

Let me back up a minute and give you the pre-story story. About a year before this incident, Alex had sent me a desperate text at 4:30 a.m. He explained how he had disconnected from an abusive church leader and needed a place of refuge. Since I had escaped a church like the one he described ten years earlier, my heart went out to him. I helped Alex walk through some emotional healing, and he was making fast progress. I was proud of him.

Some months later, Alex asked me to write a book with him on a topic I had been teaching in-depth for a couple of years. He had some strong revelations on the subject, and I was impressed. Although I was hesitant to take on another project—I was traveling to Europe every month and had a book deadline looming—he convinced me to come alongside him to publish the book that would carry both our names.

The truth accidentally came out shortly before the coauthored book was completely edited. (Doesn't it always?) I was in a phone meeting with our publisher to discuss marketing plans for the upcoming coauthored title. Out of nowhere—it had to be the Holy Spirit—the publisher revealed Alex had pitched a homerun book idea and had just signed a second contract. She thought I would be proud, but I did not feel proud. I felt betrayed. I was betrayed.

Alex went behind my back and presented as his own a book idea I had shared with him in confidence—as if I wouldn't find out when it hit the store shelves. That's called intellectual property theft. When I told the publisher Alex robbed the concept from me, they immediately canceled his contract. But the damage was done. He demonstrated a serious character flaw and was not the least bit apologetic about it. He was deceived.

FROM THEFT TO THEFT

Since I had written over 80 percent of the "coauthored" book and rewritten the small portions Alex did contribute, I told the publisher we could not move forward with his name on the book. I didn't want my good name forever associated with his on the cover of what was bound to be a bestseller. The publisher agreed and canceled Alex's contract due to plagiarism.

What Alex did next still shocks me. He took the original content I wrote for the coauthored book and self-published it with his name as the sole author, even though the same content was scheduled to be published with my name on it within months. He also got a popular minister to endorse his plagiarized book unknowingly. Of course, with that endorsement, his book (which was really my book) became an instant hit. After the shock wore off, the anger set in.

It was a double whammy. To make matters worse, Alex worked overtime to convince everyone he was a victim and I was lying. I had to walk through a painstaking process with my publisher to prove the content was mine, even though it was clear the writing styles were vastly different. I have been writing professionally for three decades. His storytelling, grammar, and style didn't match.

But wait, there's more. The copycat also manipulated the popular minister who had endorsed his book. This anointed woman vehemently defended Alex despite our long-standing relationship and my widespread reputation as a journalist, Christian author, and editor of *Charisma* magazine. At that point, my emotions went beyond shock to hurt—and it dragged out for weeks before my publisher finally sent Alex a cease-and-desist order. The book was removed from online stores.

But the drama didn't stop there. Alex threatened to sue the publisher for canceling his contract. At the end of the day, the publisher went forward with my content, and we published the original book with only my name on it. It became a bestseller. I later published the book idea Alex tried to steal, and it also became a bestseller. I was invited on many television shows, and it helped further establish my voice on the topic. What the enemy meant for harm, God turned for good (Gen. 50:20). God vindicated me with icing on top.

WHAT IS DOUBLE VINDICATION?

My experience with Alex ended with double for my trouble. I call it double vindication, and I've seen it manifest in my life many times. You too can tap into double vindication. Double vindication is scriptural.

Isaiah 61:7 promises: "Instead of your shame you shall have double honor, and instead of confusion they shall rejoice in their portion. Therefore in their land they shall possess double; everlasting joy shall be theirs." *The Message* puts it this way: "Because you got a double dose of trouble and more than your share of contempt, your inheritance in the land will be doubled and your joy go on forever." Amen.

God can bring double vindication in any area of your life. He can "double vindicate" you from poor treatment. He can "double vindicate" you in the face of false accusations. He can "double vindicate" you from greedy, vindictive people. He can "double vindicate" you when someone steals from you. He can "double vindicate" you from the enemy attack. God is not just your vindicator. He is your double vindicator just like He was Job's double vindicator.

Think about it. Job went through one of the worst trials we see in Scripture. But in the end, he got double vindication.

Job 42:12–17 tells us: "Now the LORD blessed the latter days of Job more than his beginning; for he had fourteen thousand sheep, six thousand camels, one thousand yoke of oxen, and one thousand female donkeys. He also had seven sons and three daughters. And he called the name of the first Jemimah, the name of the second Keziah, and the name of the third Keren-Happuch. In all the land were found no women so beautiful as the daughters of Job; and their father gave them an inheritance among their brothers. After this Job lived one hundred and forty years, and saw his children and grandchildren for four generations. So Job died, old and full of days."

Think of Rachel. She was barren and desperate to have children—and barrenness was seen as a curse in her time. She was so envious of her sister Leah that she said to her husband, Jacob, "Give me children, or else I die!" (Gen. 30:1) Rachel was seeking vindication but wasn't willing to wait on God. She gave Jacob her maid, Bilhah, to have relations with, and he bore a son. "Rachel named him Dan, for she said, 'God has vindicated me! He has heard my request and given me a son'" (Gen. 30:6, NLT).

Rachel was willing to settle for what I call sideways vindication. But this was not true vindication any more than Ishmael was Abraham's promised son. Like Sarah and Abraham, Rachel had to wait to see true vindication. Finally, in Genesis 30:22–24, we read: "Then God remembered Rachel, and God listened to her and opened her womb. And she conceived and bore a son, and said, 'God has taken away my reproach.' So she called his name Joseph, and said, "The LORD shall add to me another son."

Joseph ended up saving the entire world from a seven-year famine with a prophetic strategy. Rachel had more than vindication. She got double vindication when Benjamin was born. But note that Rachel declared, "The LORD shall add to me another son." She was standing for double vindication.

TAPPING INTO DOUBLE VINDICATION

So what's the common denominator between Job and Rachel? How did these biblical figures tap into double vindication? Simply stated, through prayer. See, you can't just assume double vindication will manifest on its own. Even though God is your vindicator, He expects us to pray. So if you need vindication, pray for vindication. Better yet, pray for double vindication.

David prayed, "Vindicate me, O LORD, for I have walked in my integrity, and I have trusted in the LORD without wavering" (Ps. 26:1, ESV). And again, "Vindicate me, O God, and plead my case against an ungodly nation; oh, deliver me from the deceitful and unjust man!" (Ps. 43:1). And again, "Save me, O God, by Your name, and vindicate me by Your power" (Ps. 54:1, NASB). David didn't wait on the promise of vindication to chase him down and overtake him. He prayed it in.

I did the same thing. It was a double betrayal when Alex swiped both my content and my new book idea. I knew I had to pray for Alex, his endorser, as well as the publisher, and put the matter in God's hands. I could see the enemy's plan to steal a hundred hours of work, ruin relationships, and block new opportunities if God didn't intervene. So I prayed for vindication. I prayed for justice. I prayed the lies would be exposed. And, yes, I prayed and blessed Alex.

Job, too, prayed. When you find yourself under attack, sometimes even the people closest to you will suggest you've done something to open a door to the enemy in your life. Indeed, many of our best friends suddenly turn into "Job's friends." You know what I mean. Eliphaz comes over to your house to tell you how it's all your fault because you have some hidden sin in your life (Job 4:7–8). After he leaves, Bildad calls to confirm Eliphaz's poor prophecies (Job 8:20). Finally, Zophar acts as a third witness to condemn you in the battle (Job 11:14–17).

Indeed, we all have plenty of friends who like to judge us when life isn't going our way. The enemy uses those close to us to add poison to his fiery darts when what we need is someone to stand in the gap for us. Of course, we should all examine our hearts when the onslaught comes to make sure we don't have any open doors, but too many well-intentioned Christians give pat answers and platitudes that do not reflect God's heart in the midst of our battle.

A LESSON FROM JOB

Job's self-defense didn't bring double vindication. Job's complaints didn't bring him double vindication. No, Job didn't get double vindication until he prayed for his friends. It turns out God wasn't too happy with the way they treated him. Look at Job 42:7–8:

> And so it was, after the LORD had spoken these words to Job, that the LORD said to Eliphaz the Temanite, "My wrath is aroused against you and your two friends, for you have not spoken of Me what is right, as My servant Job has. Now therefore, take for yourselves seven bulls and seven rams, go to My servant Job, and offer up for yourselves a burnt offering; and My servant Job shall pray for you. For I will accept him, lest I deal with you according to

your folly; because you have not spoken of Me what
is right, as My servant Job has."

Now look at Job 42:10–11 to see how Job activated the
double vindication:

> And the LORD restored Job's losses when he prayed
> for his friends. Indeed the LORD gave Job twice as
> much as he had before. Then all his brothers, all
> his sisters, and all those who had been his acquain-
> tances before, came to him and ate food with him
> in his house; and they consoled him and comforted
> him for all the adversity that the LORD had brought
> upon him. Each one gave him a piece of silver and
> each a ring of gold.

David understood how to pray for vindication. You can
personalize this prayer from Psalm 31:16–20 (NLT):

> Let your favor shine on your servant. In your
> unfailing love, rescue me. Don't let me be dis-
> graced, O LORD, for I call out to you for help. Let
> the wicked be disgraced; let them lie silent in the
> grave. Silence their lying lips—those proud and
> arrogant lips that accuse the godly.
>
> How great is the goodness you have stored up
> for those who fear you. You lavish it on those who
> come to you for protection, blessing them before
> the watching world. You hide them in the shelter of
> your presence, safe from those who conspire against
> them. You shelter them in your presence, far from
> accusing tongues.

CHAPTER 29

WALKING IN CONSISTENT VINDICATION

WAS PREPARING TO speak to ten thousand hungry people when my host peeked in with what she thought was exciting news. A well-known minister was at the event and was waiting to hear me speak. Of course, the host did not know this man had cursed me publicly and spread vicious lies about me. My host thought I'd be excited to meet him.

With this news, my adrenaline started flowing. Why was he here? What was his motive? Was he there to inti-mate me? Was he there to disrupt the meeting? Was he telling lies about me to the host? Was he going to curse me while I was preaching? My imagination was running wild, so I started praying.

During worship, I turned my attention from the man and onto the Lord—and He gave me a clear strategy: bless him—and do it publicly. I blessed the man and broke curses off his life in front of ten thousand people. Yes, really. The man broke down in tears, and we've been good friends ever since. In that experience, I saw firsthand how God can turn the curse into a blessing.

(See Deuteronomy 23:5.) And it was yet another example of how vindication is the story of my life.

When something is your "life's story," it means it's a consistent theme. To be sure, vindication is a consistent theme in my life. I'll admit it. I don't always immediately rejoice when I am wronged. Sometimes it takes me a few hours—or a few days—to process what happened. But soon enough, I end up with a big smile on my face when someone wrongs me because I know vindication is my portion.

Vindication is your portion too. But remember, if you want to walk in consistent vindication, you need to stay on the right side of God through the waiting. That means more than forgiving those who wronged you, blessing those who curse you, and praying for those who despitefully use you. It means more than avoiding self-vindication.

Walking in consistent vindication demands not fretting over the evil done to you. Walking in consistent vindication demands learning to rejoice in the midst of your suffering. Walking in consistent vindication demands not gloating when your enemies fall flat on their faces. If you walk this way, you'll see God avenge you of your enemies every time.

STOP FRETTING!

When I see people who I know are dealing falsely, it grieves me. But I don't fret about it. I've worked with Christian businesses that are clearly money motivated and treat their employees poorly, but I refuse to fret. I've seen evil people manipulate their way into promotions and platforms, but I choose not to fret.

You can't walk in faith for vindication and walk in fret at the same time. Fretting means "to eat or gnaw into... corrode, to cause to suffer emotional strain...agitate... grate...become vexed or worried."[1] As you can see, fretting is not compatible with being in faith for vindication. When we are fretting it, we're not "faithing it."

Here is Paul's time-tested advice: "Don't fret or worry. Instead of worrying, pray. Let petitions and praises shape your worries into prayers, letting God know your concerns. Before you know it, a sense of God's wholeness, everything coming together for good, will come and settle you down. It's wonderful what happens when Christ displaces worry at the center of your life" (Phil. 4:6–7, MSG).

Fretting is akin to frustration. It can be frustrating to watch people advance at your expense, whether financially, relationally, or career-wise. Surely you've read the scripture, "Casting all your care upon Him, for He cares for you" (1 Pet. 5:7). What is a frustration, ultimately, but a care? What would happen if, instead of frustrating the grace of God in our lives, we cast the frustrations and tapped into the grace instead?

When you are frustrated with your boss for not giving you that promotion, why not pray: "Father, I'm grateful that I have a job and that You are my provider. I trust You for the right promotion at the right time, and I believe you for increase in my life."

Instead of acting in frustration with your kids, why not pray to God instead? When you do, the second half of Philippians 4:7 can manifest in your life: "The peace of

God, which surpasses all understanding, will protect your hearts and minds through Christ Jesus" (MEV). When you are peaceful, you can receive abundant grace while you wait for vindication.

BEWARE OF GLOATING

If you stand in faith, your vindication will come. It's inevitable. The people who wronged you may not be able to repay you or otherwise make it right, but God will make the crooked places straight. (See Isaiah 45:2.) God will repay you. And when He does, don't gloat.

Solomon offered some strategic advice: "Do not rejoice when your enemy falls, and do not let your heart be glad when he stumbles; lest the LORD see it, and it displease Him, and He turn away His wrath from him" (Prov. 24:17–18). And Proverbs 17:5 emphasizes, "He who is glad at calamity will not go unpunished." That's heavy motivation not to gloat!

Toward the end of his anguishing trial, Job demonstrated this principle. He clearly understood the danger of rejoicing at his enemy's downfall. He cried out to God in prayer just in case he had transgressed in this area. We see his prayer in Job 31:29–30: "If I have rejoiced at the destruction of him who hated me, or lifted myself up when evil found him (indeed I have not allowed my mouth to sin by asking for a curse on his soul)."

David prayed a similar prayer in Psalm 7:3–5: "O LORD my God, if I have done this: If there is iniquity in my hands, if I have repaid evil to him who was at peace with me, or have plundered my enemy without cause, let the enemy pursue me and overtake me; yes, let him trample my life to the earth, and lay my honor in the dust. Selah."

When Saul died, David didn't rejoice. David had cried out for vindication for years and years—and years—while running from Saul in the wilderness. When the ultimate vindication finally came—when God removed Saul from the throne to make room for David—he didn't throw a party and dance on Saul's grave.

Quite the contrary, 2 Samuel 1 says David lamented over Saul and Jonathan and even wrote a song to honor their memory. Here's the thing. It's not a matter of *if* your enemy will stumble but *when* he will stumble if he doesn't repent. Don't rejoice when your enemy stumbles. Continue to pray for them. Move in the opposite spirit so you can walk in consistent vindication.

REJOICE IN THE SUFFERING

Job went through radical suffering. He lost his sheep, his oxen, his camels—which were essentially his finances—his servants, and every one of his sons and daughters. Finally, he lost his health—and I imagine he almost lost his mind. This illustrates how the enemy brings suffering in four primary areas of our life: our minds, our relationships, our finances, and our bodies.

Consider the definition of suffering. Suffering means to be forced to endure. When suffering comes your way, you are forced to endure it. What is the alternative? What choice do you have? You may as well rejoice now in faith that God will vindicate you later.

Paul wrote, "Not only that, but we rejoice in our sufferings, knowing that suffering produces endurance, and endurance produces character, and character produces hope, and hope does not put us to shame, because God's love has been poured into our hearts through the Holy Spirit who has been given to us" (Rom. 5:3–5, ESV).

Peter offered, "In this you rejoice, though now for a little while, if necessary, you have been grieved by various trials, so that the tested genuineness of your faith— more precious than gold that perishes though it is tested by fire—may be found to result in praise and glory and honor at the revelation of Jesus Christ" (1 Pet. 1:6–7, ESV).

And James put it this way, "Count it all joy, my brothers, when you meet trials of various kinds, for you know that the testing of your faith produces steadfastness. And let steadfastness have its full effect, that you may be perfect and complete, lacking in nothing" (Jas. 1:2–4, ESV).

Rejoice, not just because you are walking in consistent vindication. Rejoice because the suffering is conforming you into the image of Christ. While you rejoice instead of fretting in the face of wrongdoing against you, you'll produce character and endurance, and the next time you're wronged, you won't be so quick to fall into self-pity or anger. You won't seek self-vindication. You'll fall more in love with the God who vindicates you.

CHAPTER 30

YOUR VINDICATION TESTIMONY

I F MY VINDICATION story blessed you, yours will surely bless someone else. Your testimony can breathe hope into someone who's been beaten up and torn down. Indeed, your story can encourage someone to stand in faith while waiting for God's vindication.

Think about it. Don't vindication testimonies in Scripture inspire your faith? Daniel was vindicated in the lion's den. Shadrach, Meshach, and Abednego were vindicated in the fiery furnace (Dan. 3). Job was vindicated when he prayed for his friends. Jesus was vindicated by the Father.

David's vindication testimony was based on a lifetime of following God through pain and suffering, trials and tribulations, victory—and vindication. He wrote in Psalm 37:25–26, "I have been young, and now am old; yet I have not seen the righteous forsaken, nor his descendants begging bread. He is ever merciful, and lends; and his descendants are blessed."

What's your vindication story? If you don't have one yet, you will when you put what you've learned in this book into practice and wait on the Lord.

WHY VINDICATION TESTIMONIES ARE CRITICAL

God's Word encourages us to share our testimonies. Peter put it this way: "Honor the Messiah as Lord in your hearts. Always be ready to give a defense to anyone who asks you for a reason for the hope that is in you" (1 Pet. 3:15, HCSB). Our testimonies inspire hope in the hearts of those who are going through hard times—and even those who don't know the Lord. David said, "I will tell of your name to my brothers; in the midst of the congregation I will praise you" (Ps. 22:22, ESV).

Someone needs to hear your story. They may be going through the exact same trial you've overcome. I can't tell you how many people weep and cry when they hear how I rebuilt a better life after my husband ran out on me. For recently abandoned or divorced women, my vindication story shows them what's possible. Likewise, many people who have gone to jail or prison find hope in my story because God restored my life and gave me far more than double for my trouble. David said, "Come and hear, all you who fear God, and I will tell what he has done for my soul" (Ps. 66:16, ESV).

Let's be real. People love stories. It's scientifically proven that we learn and retain information through stories. Stories intrigue us. That's why we like to go to movies and read books or watch television. Your testimony is your story. And your story will touch and move people's hearts to believe in God and His Word for vindication. Ultimately, your vindication testimony both gives glory to God and builds faith in God as the vindicator. It's a win-win.

Your testimony becomes a story about the character of God and the ways of God. David said, "I have proclaimed the good news of righteousness in the great assembly; indeed, I do not restrain my lips, O LORD, You Yourself know. I have not hidden Your righteousness within my heart; I have declared Your faithfulness and Your salvation; I have not concealed Your lovingkindness and Your truth from the great assembly" (Ps. 40:9–10).

HOW TO GIVE YOUR VINDICATION TESTIMONY

Psalm 107:1–2 tells us, "Oh, give thanks to the LORD, for He is good! For His mercy endures forever. Let the redeemed of the LORD say so, whom He has redeemed from the hand of the enemy."

I remember the first time I was asked to give a testimony in church. I had no idea how to go about that, but, thankfully, a sister in Christ gave me some guidelines: start by glorifying God, then tell about the breakthrough, then thank those who God used to help you.

Vindication is life-transforming, so when you give your testimony, you want to give a brief account of how you were wronged. What happened? You don't need to give every gory detail, but you need to paint a picture of the dire situation in such a way that people know only God could have vindicated you. Explain how you prayed. Explain how you stayed in faith when it looked impossible.

Once you've painted this picture through your story-telling, spend some time sharing how God made a way out of no way. Explain how God showed up and showed out. Tell the story of exactly how He vindicated you. What was the outcome of your prayer, faith, and waiting?

Then talk about what your life looks like now. How did the vindication have a lasting effect? How did it impact your relationship with God?

While you are sharing, don't start preaching. Use words like "I" and "me." The story is about you. Don't mention the names of people, churches, or businesses that wronged you. In fact, mask them completely if you can. Use informal language and be super honest about your struggles. Act like you are talking to a friend. Don't go back too far in time. People will lose interest. Keep it pertinent to one vindication. Always wrap up by giving glory to God.

David wrote in Psalm 71:15–17: "My mouth shall tell of Your righteousness and Your salvation all the day, for I do not know their limits. I will go in the strength of the Lord GOD; I will make mention of Your righteousness, of Yours only. O God, You have taught me from my youth; and to this day I declare Your wondrous works."

Ask God for opportunities to testify. He knows who needs to hear your story.

NOTES

CHAPTER 1

1. "Marcus Aurelius Quotes," Good Reads, accessed April 19, 2024, https://www .goodreads.com/quotes/186784-the-best-revenge-is-to-be-unlike-him-who-performed.
2. Ray C. Stedman, "Let God Be God: The Wrong of Self-Defense," Ray Stedman Ministries, accessed March 4, 2024, https:// www.raystedman.org/old-testament/job/the-wrong-of-self-defense.
3. Francis Bacon, *The Essays or Counsels, Civil and Moral* (London: John Haviland, 1632), 21.
4. Francis Bacon, "Of Revenge," CommonLit, accessed March 4, 2024, https://www .commonlit.org/en/texts/on-revenge.
5. Oswald Chambers, "The Distraction of Contempt," *My Utmost for His Highest*, November 23, https://utmost.org/the-distraction-of-contempt/.

CHAPTER 2

1. Joel Osteen, *I Declare* (New York: FaithWords, 2012), 10–11.

CHAPTER 5

1. Blue Letter Bible, s.v. *"agape,"* accessed May 18, 2024, https://www.blueletterbible.org/lexicon/g25/nkjv/tr/0-1/.
2. Martin Luther King Jr., *Strength to Love* (Boston: Beacon Press, 1963), 47.

CHAPTER 6

1. Henry Cloud, *Changes That Heal* (Grand Rapids, MI: Zondervan, 1992), 194.
2. Merriam-Webster.com, s.v. "magnify," accessed May 9, 2024, https://www.merriam-webster.com/dictionary/magnify#:~:text=%3A%20to%20cause%20to%20be%20held,to%20increase%20in%20significance%20%3A%20intensify.

CHAPTER 7

1. Blue Letter Bible, s.v. *"qārā',"* accessed April 18, 2024, https://www.blueletterbible.org/lexicon/h7121/kjv/wlc/0-1/.
2. Bible Study Tools, s.v. *"tsarach,"* accessed April 18, 2024, https://www.biblestudytools.com/lexicons/hebrew/nas/tsarach.html#google_vignette.

CHAPTER 8

1. Merriam-Webster.com, s.v. "decree," accessed May 18, 2024, https://www.merriam-webster.com/dictionary/decree.

CHAPTER 9

1. "Some Quotations on Slander From the Puritans," Memoir and Remains, September 28, 2018, https://memoirandremains .com/2018/09/28/some-quotations-on-slander-from-the-puritans/.

CHAPTER 10

1. Merriam-Webster.com, s.v. "coup," accessed April 18, 2024, https://www.merriam-webster.com/dictionary/coup.
2. Fanny Lalot, "The Unkindest Cut of All: A Quantitative Study of Betrayal Narratives," *Journal of Applied Social Psychology* 33, no. 6 (November/December 2023): 1580–1601, https://doi.org/10.1002/casp.2738.
3. "10 Spurgeon Quotes for Dealing with Betrayal," The Spurgeon Center, September 29, 2016, https://www.spurgeon.org/resource-library/blog-entries/10-spurgeon-quotes-for-dealing-with-betrayal/#:~:text=deceive%20your%20trust.%E2%80%9D-,%E2%80%9CIf%20you%20will%20trust%20yourselves%20with%20the%20Saviour%2C%20he%20cannot,(MTP%2024%3A204).

CHAPTER 11

1. Bible Study Tools, s.v. "2 Timothy 4:14," accessed April 18, 2024, https://www.biblestudytools.com/commentaries/

gills-exposition-of-the-bible/2-timothy-4-14
.html#:~:text=It%20was%20very%20
likely%20he,show%20the%20insolence%20
of%20the.

2. Charmain Hibberd, "Do Yourself a Favour
   and Forgive," CBN.com, February 12,
   2018, https://www.cbneurope.com/blogs/
   do-yourself-a-favour-and-forgive/.

CHAPTER 12

1. Ralph Waldo Emerson, *The Essay on Self-
   Reliance* (East Aurora, NY: The Roycrofters,
   1908).

CHAPTER 14

1. David Remnick, "The Original Truman
   Capote," *Washington Post*, August 26,
   1984, https://www.washingtonpost.com/
   archive/lifestyle/1984/08/27/the-original-
   truman-capote/e4700401-34b6-46a7-bcf9-
   6826b3ffdeea/.

2. Merriam-Webster.com, s.v. "insult," accessed
   May 19, 2024, https://www.merriam-webster
   .com/dictionary/insult.

CHAPTER 16

1. "Ronnie Long, Black Man Wrongfully
   Convicted and Imprisoned for 44 years,
   Gets $25 Million Settlement and Apology
   From City," CBS News, January 10,
   2024, https://www.cbsnews.com/news/

ronnie-long-25-million-settlement-black-
man-44-years-prison-north-carolina/.

2. Merriam-Webster.com, s.v. "assassination,"
accessed May 20, 2024, https://www
.merriam-webster.com/dictionary/
assassination.

3. "How Making an Accusation Makes You
Seem More Trustworthy," Vanderbilt
University, January 29, 2018, https://news
.vanderbilt.edu/2019/01/29/how-making-
an-accusation-makes-you-seem-more-
trustworthy/.

4. Merriam-Webster.com, s.v. "assassination."

CHAPTER 19

1. Charles Spurgeon, "Mary Magdelene,"
January 26, 1868, https://www.spurgeon
.org/resource-library/sermons/mary-
magdalene/#flipbook/.

2. Spurgeon, "Mary Magdelene."

CHAPTER 20

1. Merriam-Webster.com, s.v. "kairos," accessed
April 18, 2024, https://www.merriam-
webster.com/dictionary/kairos.

2. "Paralyzed Woman Walks Again," Facebook,
accessed April 18, 2024, https://www
.facebook.com/700club/videos/paralyzed-
woman-walks-again/10153549737496668/.

CHAPTER 22

1. Jasmine Urquhart, "Half of Black Women Believe They Will Be Overlooked for Promotions, Study Finds," February 28, 2022, https://www.peoplemanagement.co.uk/article/1751672/half-black-women-believe-they-overlooked-promotions-study-finds.
2. Matty Merritt, "Fully Remote Workers Are Missing Out on Promotions," Morning Brew, January 13, 2024, https://www.morningbrew.com/daily/stories/fully-remote-workers-are-missing-out-on-promotions.

CHAPTER 23

1. Merriam-Webster.com, s.v. "indeed," accessed May 9, 2024, https://www.merriam-webster.com/dictionary/indeed.

CHAPTER 26

1. Charles Spurgeon, "Waiting Only Upon God," August 2, 1857, The Spurgeon Center, https://www.spurgeon.org/resource-library/sermons/waiting-only-upon-god/#flipbook/.

CHAPTER 27

1. Bible Study Tools, s.v. "kairos," accessed April 19, 2024, https://www.biblestudytools.com/lexicons/greek/nas/kairos.html#:~:text=Kairos%20Definition&text=a%20fixed%20and%20

definite%20time,opportune%20or%20
seasonable%20time.

2. Bible Hub, s.v. "2540. kairos," accessed April
19, 2024, https://biblehub.com/greek/2540.htm.

CHAPTER 29

1. Merriam-Webster.com, s.v. "fret," accessed
May 23, 2024, https://www.merriam-webster
.com/dictionary/fret.

ABOUT THE AUTHOR

JENNIFER LeCLAIRE IS an internationally recognized best-selling author, teacher, and conference speaker. She carries a reforming voice that inspires and challenges believers to pursue intimacy with God, cultivate their spiritual gifts, and walk in the fullness of what God has called them to do.

Jennifer is contending for awakening in the nations through intercession and spiritual warfare, strong apostolic preaching, and practical prophetic teaching that equips the saints for the work of the ministry.

Jennifer is senior leader of Awakening House of Prayer in Fort Lauderdale, Florida, founder of the Ignite Network, and founder of the Awakening Prayer Hubs prayer movement in over one hundred nations.

Jennifer formerly served as the first-ever female editor of *Charisma* magazine. She has written over fifty books. Some of her materials have been translated into Spanish, Chinese, Portuguese, French, Dutch, and Korean.

Jennifer has a powerful testimony of God's power to set the captives free and claim beauty for ashes. She shares her story with women who need to understand the love and grace of God in a lost and dying world.

Visit Jennifer's website at www.jenniferleclaire.org.

My FREE Gift to You

DEAR READER,

Remember to rejoice, even in a season of suffering! I hope that my personal story convinced you to trust and rejoice in the Lord's presence in all circumstances. I also pray that my book provided you with the patience and the faith to know that by His own righteous standards, God will right all the wrongs done to you.

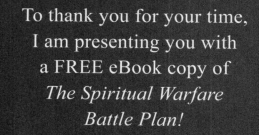

To thank you for your time, I am presenting you with a FREE eBook copy of *The Spiritual Warfare Battle Plan!*

TO REDEEM your present, please go to

≫ MyCharismaShop.com/pages/vindicated-free-gift ≪

Let the Lord Lead Your Life,

Jennifer LeClaire